The Great Canadian Quiz Book

The Great Canadian Quiz Book

Paul Russell

Gage Publishing • Agincourt

Gage Publishing
Copyright © Paul Russell, 1977
No part of this book may be used in any form
without permission in writing from the publisher.

ISBN 0-7715-9390-2 bd
ISBN 0-7715-9391-0 pa

Designed by Fortunato Aglialoro
Illustrations by Roy Condy

Printed and bound in Canada
1 2 3 4 5 JD 81 80 79 78 77

Acknowledgements:

Over the years, many people have contributed formats and ideas for questions on CBC's TV quiz show "Reach For The Top," which appear in this book. I would like to thank Sandy Stewart, executive producer of the show, for his help and advice on this project; Bill Guest, host of the national series; researchers Cliff Arnold, Barbara Collier and Doug Lavender and Alan Walker, editor on the show, for his sardonic though often witty suggestions.

Paul Russell
July 27, 1977

Introduction

It's difficult to fire the imagination on a subject, without having a few facts on hand. Facts and figures – old fashioned memory work – are the building blocks of thought, of creative imaginings. Canada has a background of facts and figures, which are much more complex than most of us realize. Some are crucial; some trivial; all are interesting. As a sum total, they are the image of Canada in the minds of people around the world. For Canada is more than a large chunk of the globe's surface, it's also a concept, created by people who think about the facts and figures of its history, geography and culture. This book holds but a few of them.

Paul Russell

Cross-Canada Quiz

This is a book packed with information – facts you might have
forgotten, and many that will be new. Let's start off with a trip
across Canada.

Q "From Sea to Shining Sea" is the curious English
translation for what?

> *A Mari usque ad Mare ("shining" is omitted in the Latin text)*

Q This is a travel book – we will start at one "mare" and
continue to the other – quick! Approximately how many
miles is that?

> *Six thousand*

Q The journey begins in the East – to be specific, at the most
easterly point of the mainland in North America. Can you
name it?

> *Cape Spear*

Q It's also the most easterly point on the island known as?

> *Newfoundland*

Q This island is a province – with additional territories on the
mainland – called what?

> *Labrador*

Q Labrador and Newfoundland boast airports called Goose and Gander. Which is on the island?

⇨ *Gander*

Q The capital of Newfoundland was traditionally founded on June 24, 1483. Whose feast day is that?

⇨ *St. John's*

Q Newfoundland is proud of its elk – what is their more common name on the mainland?

⇨ *Moose*

Q Are there icebergs off the coast of Newfoundland in June?.

⇨ *Yes*

Q Who is Newfoundland's "Father of Confederation"?

⇨ *Joey Smallwood*

Q What foreign country has possessions closest to Newfoundland?

⇨ *France*

Q When did France give up its claims to Newfoundland?

⇨ *1713*

Q Are there icebergs off the coast of Newfoundland in July?

⇨ *Yes*

Q What was the name of Newfoundland's most famous train?

⇨ *The Newfie Bullet*

Q Are there icebergs off the coast of Newfoundland in August?

⇨ *Yes*

Q What is Newfoundland's most famous domestic animal?

⇨ *Newfoundland Dog*

Q What kind of dog is associated with Labrador?

⇨ *Retriever*

Q What strait separates Newfoundland and Labrador?

⇨ *Strait of Belle Isle*

Q The great white fleet makes an annual visit to St. John's harbor – from what country?

⇨ *Portugal (the Portuguese fishing fleet has used St. John's as a supply base continuously since about 1500)*

3

Q Halfway between Portugal and Newfoundland lie what islands?

▷ *Azores*

Q From Newfoundland, it's a short ferryboat ride to Nova Scotia, or as the French used to call it–?

▷ *Acadia*

Q The flag of Nova Scotia is distinguished by a blue cross. It's the cross of which saint?

▷ *Saint Andrew*

Q Everyone knows the capital of the province is Halifax, but what was the Indian name for Halifax's important location?

▷ *Chebucto*

Q What does Chebucto mean?

▷ *Chief Harbour*

Q One of Halifax's most famous inhabitants was the Duke of Kent. Who was his most famous daughter?

▷ *Queen Victoria*

Q Do you remember Anna and the King of Siam? She lived in Halifax after her eastern trip, and continued to work as a–?

▷ *Schoolteacher*

4

Q Name the road link between Cape Breton Island and mainland Nova Scotia.

▷ *Canso Causeway*

Q Can you name the famous scenic highway that skirts Cape Breton Island?

▷ *Cabot Trail*

Q What mineral is usually associated with Cape Breton?

▷ *Coal*

Q Cape Breton Island was also the location of France's most important Atlantic bastion – in the 18th century. Can you name it?

▷ *Louisbourg*

Q When did Louisbourg fall to the British – for the last time?

▷ *1758*

Q What is the present population of Louisbourg?

▷ *Approximately 1600*

Q Can you name the large "basin" of deep water in Halifax used by the Atlantic convoy fleets of World War I I?

▷ *Bedford Basin (At 6 sq. miles it is big enough and deep enough to accommodate the combined navies of the world.)*

Q Now we move from Nova Scotia to the province of the reversing falls. Can you name it?

▷ *New Brunswick*

Q The Reversing Falls of the Saint John River is caused by what phenomenon in the Bay of Fundy?

▷ *Tidal bore (The tides in the Bay of Fundy are the highest tides on earth. When the tide washes landward, it flows up rivers apparently reversing their flow.)*

Q In what province would I find "Push and be Damned" Rapids?

▷ *New Brunswick*

Q The first cathedral of the Anglican communion to be built since the Norman Conquest in a new location, was constructed in what Canadian city?

▷ *Fredericton*

Q Who was the "Prince Edward" referred to in the name of Canada's smallest province, Prince Edward Island?

▷ *Edward, Duke of Kent, father of Queen Victoria*

Q The Trans-Canada highway wanders northwest from Fredericton to the Quebec border and meets the St. Lawrence river at what city?

▷ *Rivière du Loup*

6

Q What does that name mean in English?

⇨ *River of the wolf*

Q What is the old Indian name for the original site of Quebec City?

⇨ *Stadacona (Jacques Cartier visited there in 1535)*

Q What is the popular French Canadian idiom for the St. Lawrence river?

⇨ *Le Fleuve (meaning "the river that flows to the sea")*

Q Who founded Quebec City?

⇨ *Champlain*

Q Quebec City used to have a French governor's palace at the brow of the cliff. What building now stands on the old vice-regal site?

⇨ *Château Frontenac (a large railway hotel)*

Q What is the highest mountain peak in the province of Quebec?

⇨ *Mount Jacques Cartier (also called Table Top Mountain, 4,160 ft. high)*

Q Which Canadian city is called "The Gibraltar of North America"?

⇨ *Quebec City*

Q Which Canadian water canal allows ships to overcome the 326-foot drop between levels of Lakes Erie and Ontario?

⇨ *Welland Canal*

Q "Beautiful Lake" is the translation of the Huron Indian name for which Canadian province?

⇨ *Ontario ("Ontare" means lake; "io" means beautiful)*

Q Ninety-five percent of the western world's known output of what mineral is mined in Ontario's Sudbury district?

⇨ *Nickel*

Q Which Canadian city was formerly called Fort Rouge and Fort Garry, and whose current name roughly means the Cree phrase for "murky water"?

⇨ *Winnipeg (also called "The Chicago of the Canadian West")*

Q What is the most distinguishing feature of Saskatchewan's prairie lake, Little Manitou?

⇨ *It is a salt-water lake*

Q Which two Canadian provinces do not border on salt water?

⟩ *Alberta & Saskatchewan*

Q Alberta's oil-saturated tar sands stretch for more than 100 miles along which river?

⟩ *Athabasca*

Q Which west-coast city was named after a German nobleman as the result of a contest?

⟩ *Prince Rupert (named after Rupert of the Rhine, in a contest in 1906 for a western terminus for the Grand Trunk Pacific Railway)*

Q What is British Columbia's highest mountain peak?

⟩ *Mt. Fairweather (15,300 ft.)*

Q What is Canada's most westerly point?

⟩ *Mount Logan, Yukon Territory*

Q Which Canadian city recorded the lowest temperature for the Yukon Territory at 83° below zero?

⟩ *Snag (in 1947)*

Famous Canadians

Q Who was the founder of Canada's first mail-order business?

⟹ *Timothy Eaton (1834-1907). Born in 1834, a farmer's son in County Antrim, Ireland, he came to Canada in 1854. He ran a general store at St. Mary's, Upper Canada. In 1868, Timothy moved to Toronto, and entered the dry goods business. He founded a company that instituted two practices which were then unknown: he sold for cash, and at a fixed price. It is said that he revolutionized the commercial world of his time. His catalogue and mail-order business gave people in pioneer farming communities access to a variety of merchandise they could not otherwise have obtained. While doing that, he built up one of the largest family-owned businesses in the world.*

Q Who discovered insulin?

⟹ *Sir Frederick Grant Banting and Charles H. Best. Their names are rarely mentioned singly – always together, because of the importance of their tremendous discovery. Diabetes was called the wasting sickness and there was no known cure for this worldwide killer until Banting and Best began their research at the medical laboratories of the University of Toronto in 1921.*

Q What is diabetes?

⟹ *Diabetes is a disorder of the carbohydrate metabolism resulting from insufficient production, or utilization of insulin. Insulin is a hormone secreted by the pancreas, which regulates the sugar (glucose) metabolism. Abnormally high levels of glucose in the blood associated with a deficiency in the secretion of insulin (diabetes mellitus) may cause a variety of disturbances of the nervous system. Some symptoms are increased thirst, urine loss, itching, weight loss and weakness.*

11

Q Which Canadian artist is famous for her paintings of totem poles?

▷ *Emily Carr (1871–1945). She was born in Victoria, B.C. on December 13th, 1871, and spent most of her life on the West Coast, often visiting the Indian villages–a subject that was of lifelong interest. Discouraged by adverse criticism, Emily quit painting for fifteen years, but returned to it after meeting Lawren Harris and other painters of the Group of Seven. Her paintings are represented in all the major Canadian collections, and she has been ranked as one of Canada's best and most original painters.*

Q Which Canadian cleric, educator and writer wrote *Advantages of Imperial Federation* (1889), and a famous travel book entitled *Ocean to Ocean* (1873; reprinted 1925)?

▷ *George Monro Grant (1835–1902)*

Q Who was the oldest Canadian who ever lived?

▷ *In all likelihood, it was Pierre Joubert, a Quebec bootmaker, born July 15, 1701, and died Nov. 16, 1814. He was 113 years, 124 days old. This is the greatest authenticated age– greater ages have been claimed for other people, but these claims are without proper proof.*

Q Were the Smith Brothers on the cough drop box real people?

▷ *Yes, they actually lived. Their names were William and Andrew, sons of James Smith of St. Armand, Quebec. Their father received the formula for the cough candy from a journeyman, who stopped at Smith's newly opened restaurant. After their father died, the boys continued the business under the name Smith Brothers. To protect their product, the brothers decided to use their own pictures as a trademark!*

Q MacDonalds and Macdonalds and McDonalds are everywhere in Canada – we all know who Sir John A. Macdonald was – but what about James Edward Hervey MacDonald?

▷ *Well he's better known as J.E.H. MacDonald. Still don't know? He was one of the more famous members of the Group of Seven – a band of artists who developed a distinct style of painting the Canadian landscape in the early years of the 20th century. J.E.H. was born in 1873 in Durham, England and came to Canada in 1887. As a student in Hamilton, Ontario, he studied at the Hamilton Art School, then moved to Toronto to join the staff of Grip Ltd., a commercial art firm in 1895. At Grip, he met other members of what eventually became the Group of Seven. But in the early decades of this century, Canadians had very conservative tastes, and his painting "The Tangled Garden" aroused a storm of criticism when it went on view in 1916. But in the next five years MacDonald's painting and that of his colleagues, which concentrated on the wild landscapes of northern Ontario, in Algonquin Park and the Algoma district, ultimately won acceptance. The works of J.E.H. MacDonald were hung in the National Gallery, before the artist died in 1932.*

Q Who invented the telephone – and also experimented with airplanes, hydrofoils, etc.?

▷ *Alexander Graham Bell was the man who altered modern life with his ingenious talking machine. Bell was born in Scotland in 1847 and came to Canada with his family when he was still a young man in his early twenties. In 1870 he became a resident of the southern Ontario farming community of Brantford. That's where he conducted his early experiments with the telephone. The first telephone message went from Brantford to the nearby town of Paris, Ontario. Bell went on to receive many honours. He was awarded the Prix Volta from France in 1880 and used the thousand francs prize money to establish the Volta Laboratory Association. He moved to the city of Boston, to carry on work with the deaf and in 1877, married one of his students. A prosperous and respected member of the international scientific community, Bell moved to Washington, but kept his Canadian ties by building a summer residence at Baddeck, in Nova Scotia. Every summer the energetic inventor carried on a multitude of experiments, fascinated by such concepts as air flight and hydrofoil propulsion over water. Bell died on Aug. 2, 1922.*

Q Who am I?

He was an outstanding Canadian soldier and politician and was born in Ontario. In 1911 he was appointed Canada's Minister of National Defence. Name him.

▷ *Sir Samuel Hughes*

Q Sir Samuel was his own boss in Lindsay, Ontario. What was his business?

▷ *Editor-owner of a newspaper (the Lindsay Warder)*

Q In 1911, the prime minister made Sam Hughes his Minister of Militia and National Defence. One of his plans while holding that portfolio displeased many Canadians. Mr. Hughes wanted all Canadian boys trained for military service. It was the age at which he wanted them trained that angered many people. What age did Sir Sam suggest?

▷ *Twelve years old*

14

Q The Minister of Militia was considered eccentric, to say the least. For example, during an inspection of the training camp at Valcartier, he rode through the camp wearing a colonel's uniform and a hat that had some of the enlisted men calling him "Yankee Doodle." What do you suppose he had on his head?

▷ *A plumed hat*

Q Sir Samuel Hughes held his office throughout the war but as fate would have it, he was asked for his resignation because of a munitions scandal, only two hours before the Armistice was signed on November 11th, 1918. Who was the prime minister at the time?

▷ *Sir Robert Borden*

Q Who am I?

Clue I. I was born in 1803, and died in 1882. My first job was as a teacher in London District, Ontario (then Upper Canada).

Clue II. In 1841, I helped found Victoria College at Cobourg, becoming its first principal.

Clue III. My articles in *The British Colonist* and my "Report" published in 1846, were the source of grammar school reform for Upper Canada.

Clue IV. In my lifetime, I worked for secularization of Clergy Reserves, free general education and subsidized university education for all. I was onetime president of the Methodist General Conference, and I worked for responsible government in the Canadas.

▷ *Egerton Ryerson (March 24, 1803-Dec. 19, 1882)*

Q

Who am I?

Clue I. I am a great Canadian civil engineer and statesman, born in 1886. I entered the House of Commons as the representative for Port Arthur in 1935. My Christian names are Clarence Decatur.
Can you guess?

Clue I I. I am regarded by some historians as one of Canada's outstanding politicians, yet I wasn't Canadian born! I was born in the U.S. (in Waltham, Mass.)
Not yet?

Clue I I I. Soon after the election of 1935, I was made the Minister of Railways and Canals and Minister of Marine with the Liberal Government.
Getting warmer?

Clue IV. One of my major achievements was the creation of Trans-Canada Air Lines, today called Air Canada. I also established the C.B.C. and the National Harbours Board. In 1957, when Louis St. Laurent's Liberals were defeated in the federal election, I resigned and gave my full attention to my duties as the Chancellor of Dalhousie University (in Halifax, N.S.).
Have you finally guessed?

▷ I am C.D. Howe (1886-1960)

Q

Who am I?

Clue I. I am a Canadian, and was born in Moosomin, Saskatchewan in 1887.

Clue I I. Called the "father of the Canadian Army," I was a soldier, and rose to be a Brigadier-General in World War I, and finally a General (1944) in World War I I.

Clue III. I was a soldier, scientist and statesman. As a scientist, I laid the groundwork for the development of the cathode-ray detection finder. I also served as chairman of the National Research Council, the president of the Atomic Energy Control Board of Canada, and was co-chairman of the Canada-United States Joint Board of Defence.

Clue IV. In the 1960s, I was a strong advocate against the Columbia River Treaty, and fought hard to preserve Canada's water resources for future generations.

⇨ *(General, The Honorable) Andrew George Latta McNaughton (P.C., C.H., C.B., C.M.G., D.S.O., C.D., M.Sc., D. Eng., D.C.L., LL.D., I.D.C.)*

Q Who am I?

Clue I. I was born at Claremont, Ontario in 1877. I had little formal education and supported myself by working as a bush ranger in Algonquin Park.

Clue II. I never married. My greatest love was travelling in, and painting in Algonquin Park.

Clue III. Although I was virtually unknown in my lifetime, there is now a Memorial Gallery and Museum of Fine Art located in Owen Sound named after me.

Clue IV. Along with a group of other Canadian painters, we were known as the "Algonquin School." My death – an apparent drowning – is still a mystery.

⇨ *Thomas (Tom) John Thomson*

17

Q

Who am I?

Clue I. In 1904, I was born at Valleyfield, Quebec. The son of a storekeeper, I was educated in Montreal and Paris, and ordained in the Sulpician Order in 1930.

Clue II. I founded, for my order, a seminary at Fukuoka, Japan, where I taught philosophy from 1933 to 1939. In 1947, I was named rector of the Pontifical Canadian College in Rome.

Clue III. I was created Archbishop of Montreal in 1950, Cardinal in 1953, and in 1963, a member of the Vatican Consistorial Congress. Some would call me French Canada's leading churchman.

Clue IV. In 1967 I gave up my position as Cardinal to be a missionary-priest among lepers in Africa.

 Cardinal Paul-Emile Léger

Q

Who am I?

Clue I. I was born in Western Bay, Newfoundland, in 1883. My father was a clergyman, and my maternal grandfather was a sea-captain.

Clue II. I began my academic career as a psychologist, but in 1920 I became a lecturer in English at Victoria College, University of Toronto.

Clue III. I remained at Victoria College until I was named "Professor Emeritus" in 1953. I was awarded the Canada Council Medal in 1961.

Clue IV. I wrote seventeen books of verse, including *Brébeuf and His Brethren*. Some have called me the nearest thing to a "Poet Laureate" Canada has ever produced.

 Edwin John "Ned" Pratt (1883-1964)

Q

Who am I?

Clue I. I was born in 1827, in Scotland, where I studied engineering and surveying. I began my connection with Canadian railways shortly after coming to Canada in 1845.

Clue II. During my life, I represented Canada at various international conferences, authored a small shelf of books and scientific papers, and designed the first Canadian stamp – the three-penny beaver stamp issued April 23, 1851.

Clue III. Among my greatest works are *Railway Inventions* (1847), "A Railway to the Pacific through British Territory" (1858), *The Intercolonial* (1876), and *Canada and the British Imperial Cables* (1900).

Clue IV. In 1884, I sparked the meeting of the International Prime Meridian Conference, which led to the adoption of international standard time measurement.

 Sir Sandford Fleming

Q

When British Columbia joined the rest of Canada in 1871, one of the conditions of the merger was that the railroad should be built to the west coast. The job of finding the best route through the mountains was given to Fleming. Which pass did he survey through the Rockies – the one now used by the Canadian National Railway?

 Yellowhead Pass (said to be named after a clerk of the North West Company because of the color of his hair; he reportedly had used the pass as a cache for his furs)

Q Name one of the three passes Mr. Fleming surveyed for the Canadian *Pacific* Railway.

▷ *Kicking Horse Pass*
Rogers Pass
Eagle Pass

Q Who was Massey-Ferguson?

▷ *Actually, they were two people, Daniel Massey and Harry George Ferguson.*

Daniel Massey, who came to Canada as a four-year-old when his parents emigrated from Watertown, N.Y. in 1802, was a successful farmer. His realization of the settlers' need for tools and machines to till the rocky soil of the Canadian Shield led him to begin manufacturing simple farm implements in 1847. Daniel and his son Hart were leaders in one of mankind's greatest revolutions – changing the methods man had used to produce food for thousands of years. The business was joined in 1891 by Alanson Harris, a skilled mechanic and competitor, to form Massey-Harris Limited. At the time of this merger, this company was the biggest farm machinery business in the Empire. In 1865, the Massey Company won a 1st Grand Prize at the Paris International Exposition, and two Grand Gold Medals for farm machines. Emperor Napoleon III bought a Massey mower! The company's headquarters has been in Toronto since 1879. Hart's grandsons, Vincent and Raymond, are the most famous members of the family. Vincent Massey was Canada's first native-born Governor General before he died in 1967 and Raymond Massey is a well-known stage and movie actor.

Harry George Ferguson was a British industrialist who designed and manufactured agricultural machines, notably the Ferguson tractor. In the late Thirties, impressed by the need for a dependable, low-cost tractor, he perfected the Ferguson system of tractor-implement integration that utilized a hitch, the linkages and controls of which made the tractor and implement work as a single unit operated almost entirely from the driving seat. In 1953, Harry Ferguson Inc. merged with Massey-Harris to become Massey-Harris-Ferguson Limited; this was shortened in 1957 to Massey-Ferguson Limited. Today, Massey-Ferguson products are made in 58 factories located in 21 countries and sold in 182 countries. It is the non-Communist world's leading maker of tractors and combines, and the world headquarters are located in Toronto.

Q

Who am I?

Famous as an explorer he became the husband of 12-year-old Helen Boullé, daughter of the secretary of the King of France.

▷ *Samuel de Champlain*

Q

Considered to be North America's first frontiersman, he ventured as far west as Lake Superior and was eventually mysteriously murdered by his friends of the Huron Bear tribe.

▷ *Etienne Brûlé*

Q

He lived with the Hurons for 6 years before he managed to convert any of them to Christianity and he eventually died the death of a martyr at Iroquois hands.

▷ *Jean de Brébeuf (Father de Brébeuf)*

Q

He was a brave and boastful hunter, captured by Indians when he was 16 but he managed to survive to persuade Charles II to grant the Hudson's Bay Company its charter.

▷ *Pierre Radisson*

Canadian Actors

Q When the first Oscars were given out, three of the four best actresses were Canadian, the first being Mary Pickford. Name one of the others.

⮕ *Marie Dressler (or) Norma Shearer*

Q A frequent partner of Noel Coward, this zany lady more recently played in a movie called *Thoroughly Modern Millie*.

⮕ *Beatrice Lillie*

Q He once played Brutus at Stratford but moved to Hollywood and a bigger bonanza.

⮕ *Lorne Greene*

Q This actor gathered rave reviews in the Broadway musical *Cyrano*.

⮕ *Christopher Plummer*

Many of the personalities we've come to know in the world of entertainment are often better known by their fictitious names than they are by their genuine names:

Q This character is a cantankerous but colourful Canadian critic – and loves to tell our fellow countrymen what he thinks about them – especially the politicians. What he says

22

is usually pertinent – as well as impertinent! Michael Magee is the real McCoy – but who is his alter ego?

▷ *Fred C. Dobbs*

Q This man was born in Toronto. But when he appears on radio and TV he's introduced as the man from Parry Sound. His real name is Don Harron – what's the name of his well-known character?

▷ *Charlie Farquharson*

Q Who am I?

Clue I. I spent much of my time as a teenager in Oakville, Ontario – although I was born in Fort Garry, Manitoba in 1947.

Clue II. I attended McMaster University and left that institution holding a degree in Psychology! To some extent that has helped me in my chosen field!

Clue III. I was the first person ever to receive a Canada Council grant to study – magic! Shortly after I received it – I was on Broadway starring in the highly successful production called "The Magic Show!"

Clue IV. Not long ago – in Pasadena, California I astounded thousands in a theatre – and millions watching television – when I performed what was perhaps my greatest feat of magic up to that time! I made a massive elephant instantly vanish – and later reappear! But I'm not through yet – I have many more tricks up my sleeve!

▷ *Doug Henning!*

23

Famous Canadian Women

Q Who was the Canadian author who wrote *Roughing It in the Bush*?

⮕ *Susanna (Strickland) Moodie (1803–1885)*

Q Who was the patriotic worker who founded the "Imperial Order Daughters of the Empire"?

⮕ *Margaret (Polson) Murray (1844–1927) (on February 13, 1900)*

Q Who was the novelist who wrote *Anne of Green Gables*?

⮕ *Lucy Maud Montgomery (1874–1942) (published in 1908)*

Q Who was the first woman M.P. in Canada?

⮕ *Agnes (Campbell) MacPhail (1890–1954) (elected to the House of Commons in 1921 as United Farmers' of Ontario candidate for South East Grey riding)*

Q Who is the Canadian girl swimmer from Nova Scotia who won a silver and a bronze medal at Cali, Colombia in July, 1975?

⮕ *Nancy Garapick (of Halifax, Nova Scotia, in the 100 and 200-metre backstroke events)*

Q Who was Douglas Fairbanks' second wife, whom he married in 1920?

⮕ *Mary Pickford (born Gladys Mary Smith in Toronto in 1893)*

Q What female revivalist built the Angelus Temple in Los Angeles in 1922 as the centre of the "Four-Square Gospel"?

▷ *Aimee Semple McPherson (1890 – 1944)*

Q Who was Mary Ellen Smith?

▷ *She was an active promoter of women's political rights in Canada over 50 years ago. She was an elected member of the British Columbia legislature for several years before she was chosen to join the provincial cabinet. That was in 1921 and she was the first female cabinet minister in the British Commonwealth!*

Prominent Canadian Indians

Q Who is the internationally-known Cree folksinger, whose protest folk-songs made her famous?

▷ *Buffy Sainte-Marie (born in Saskatchewan in 1941)*

Q In an effort to remain under the British flag, which Mohawk Indian leader led his Six Nations from the U.S. into Canada in 1784?

▷ *Joseph Brant (Thayendanegea) (1742 – 1807)*

Q Which Onondaga athlete became one of North America's greatest long-distance runners during his lifetime?

▷ *Tom Longboat (Cogwagee) (he won the 15-mile Toronto Marathon 3 times in succession, and the 1907 25-mile Boston Marathon)*

Q Which Six Nations Indian poet wrote the following two books of verse: *White Wampum* and *Canadian Born*?

▷ *Pauline Johnson (Tekahionwake) (1862 – 1913)*

Q Who was the Blackfoot Indian Chief who refused to become involved in the Northwest Rebellion of 1885?

▷ *Crowfoot (Sahpo-Muxika) (1836 – 1890)*

Quotations by or about Canadians

Q What well-known western Canadian political leader, after being told that he knew nothing about farming because he was not a farmer himself, replied: "I never laid an egg either, but I know more about making an omelette than a hen does"?

▷ *T.C. (Thomas Clement) Douglas*

Q What national political figure once said to the press: "I haven't practised my French. It's just that you are starting to understand it better"?

▷ *John (George) Diefenbaker*

Q What famous father of 1934 said: "I have been chosen by God for a miracle"?

▷ *Oliva Dionne (father of the Dionne quintuplets, all girls, born May 28th, 1934)*

Q Which western politician had this to say about the Federal government: "Those people in Ottawa couldn't run a peanut stand"?

⟩ *William Andrew Cecil Bennett (former prime minister of B.C.)*

Q Which famous statesman, speaking about a well-known Canadian, said: "Lord Beaverbrook is at his very best when things are at their very worst"?

⟩ *(Sir) Winston Churchill (1874–1965)*

Canadian Prime Ministers

Q Who served the longest continuous term in office as prime minister of Canada?

⟩ *Sir Wilfrid Laurier (1896–1911) (a total of 15 years)*

Q Who was Canada's youngest prime minister, at age 46?

⟩ *Arthur Meighen (1874–1960) (prime minister: 1920–21 and 1926)*

Q Who was the first Canadian-born prime minister?

⟩ *Sir John (Joseph Caldwell) Abbott (prime minister from 1891–92, born Mar. 12, 1821 at St. Andrews, Lower Canada)*

Q Which title is granted for life to former and present prime ministers, governors general and chief justices?

⇨ *Right Honorable*

Q Where is the prime minister's official summer residence?

⇨ *Harrington Lake, Quebec (in the Gatineau Hills)*

Q Which prime minister was born in Amherst, Nova Scotia on July 2nd, 1821?

⇨ *Sir Charles Tupper*

Q Which prime minister was born in Berlin, renamed Kitchener, Ontario on December 17th, 1874?

⇨ *William Lyon Mackenzie King*

Q Which prime minister was born in Hopewell Hill, New Brunswick, on July 3rd, 1870?

⇨ *Viscount Richard Bedford Bennett*

Q Which prime minister was born in Newtonbrook, Ontario on April 23rd, 1897?

⇨ *Lester Bowles Pearson*

Q Which prime minister was born in Compton, Quebec, on February 1st, 1882?

⇨ *Louis Stephen St. Laurent*

Noted Canadian Statesmen

Q Do you know their first names?

1. 1890–1959: Last name Duplessis.

▷ *Maurice (LeNoblet)*

2. 1804–1873: Last name Howe.

▷ *Joseph*

3. 1874–1960: Last name Meighen.

▷ *Arthur*

4. 1821–1915: Last name Tupper.

▷ *(Sir) Charles (Hibbert)*

5. 1888–1967: Last name Vanier.

▷ *Georges*

Canadian Personalities

Q Who is the author of the books, *Ten Lost Years* and *Six War Years, 1939–45*?

▷ *Barry Broadfoot (born in Winnipeg in 1926)*

Q Which Canadian wrote the play *Question Time*?

▷ *Robertson Davies (a political fantasy, his 13th play)*

Q Which Canadian author remarked in his humorous book titled *Say Uncle: A Completely Uncalled-for History of the United States*: "Very little is known about the War of 1812 because the Americans lost it"?

▷ *Eric Nicol*

Q Which well-known Canadian was the winner of the 1968 Stephen Leacock Medal for Humour, and created the character "Rawhide"?

▷ *Max Ferguson*

Q What do these groups of three noted personalities have in common?

1. Alexander Mackenzie, John Joseph Caldwell Abbott and Mackenzie Bowell:

▷ *Prime Ministers of Canada*

2. Robert Knight Andras, Donald Stovel Macdonald and Marc Lalonde:

▷ *Members of the 1977 Trudeau Cabinet*

3. John J. Adams, Hector Blake and Aubrey Clapper:

▷ *N H L Hockey Players (all in the Hockey Hall of Fame)*

4. Neil Cusack of Ireland, Kathy Switzer of New York and Robert Noore of Toronto:

▷ *Marathon Runners (competed in the 1974 Boston Marathon)*

Q What fashion trademark is shared by the following: the eminent lawyer, Joseph Sedgwick; the late, former prime minister, Lester B. Pearson; and author-broadcaster, Pierre Berton?

▷ *The bow tie*

Q A Canadian, Jon Vickers, is currently one of the world's leading opera singers. What type of singing voice does Jon Vickers have?

▷ *Tenor*

Q What activity do Jim Hart, Joe Ferguson and Jim Plunkett all have in common?

▷ *All are professional football players*

Q Who won the Schenley Award as most outstanding player in the CFL in the 1976 season?

▷ *Ron Lancaster (quarterback and assistant coach for the Saskatchewan Roughrider football team)*

Q Who was the "Cape Breton Giant"?

▷ *The Cape Breton Giant was no monster, but a real living person, named Angus MacAskill. One of 13 children of a Scottish immigrant family to Nova Scotia, he weighed 500 pounds and stood seven-feet-nine when full grown. In 1849, at the age of 24, a New York showman signed him up for a five-year contract to exhibit his feats of strength on a worldwide circus tour. On his European tour, Queen Victoria was so impressed that she gave him two rings. In one of his*

31

acts, a famous midget named Tom Thumb did a dance on his left hand and was later dropped into Angus' coat pocket. He retired from show business when injured while tossing an anchor that weighed 2,000 pounds! When he died in 1863, it was said that his coffin was big enough to hold the bodies of three normal-sized men.

Geography

Q There is a country, whose name you should know, that might have been called something other than it is now, had the choice not been put to a vote. It was suggested it be called "Britannica," "Boretta," "Columbia," "Mesopelagia," and "Ursalia." Finally it was given the name meaning "a village or group of huts," a Huron-Iroquois word. What is the country?

▷ *Canada (The Indian word was actually "kanata.")*

Canada is made up of many fine cities and provinces. Let's explore a few!

Q What province do you head for if you dislike skunks, snakes, and poison ivy? It reportedly has none of these to upset you.

▷ *Newfoundland*

Q In which province does the map show the names of these centres – Alert Bay, Armstrong, Atlin and Barkerville?

▷ *British Columbia*

Q In which province do we find Canada's first Mormon Temple? It was built between 1915 and 1923 by Mormons who came to this country from Utah?

▷ *Alberta (the temple is at Cardston)*

34

Q Which of our cities has a skyline dominated by a 626-foot high tower? Its Education Centre features a sculpted exhibit called "The Family of Man," and it's famous for its trails bearing the names Glenmore, Blackfoot, Crowchild and McLeod.

▷ *Calgary*

Q Four of the Great Lakes have some shoreline on Ontario, but which one of them does not?

▷ *Lake Michigan*

Q In Canada, what is the name of the largest lake, found entirely within our borders?

▷ *Great Bear Lake*

Where Are You?

Listen to the following intriguing place names, and name the province in which each group of three is found:

Q In which province are you if you're visiting Cayuga, Chapleau and Bobcaygeon?

▷ *Ontario*

Q This time the places are Malagash, and La Have. The province?

▷ *Nova Scotia*

Q Let's look for Siegas, Shemogue and Chamcook. The province?

▷ *New Brunswick*

Q Now, where are we? The places we visit are named Pownal, Pisquid and Rustico. What is the province?

▷ *Prince Edward Island*

Q Here comes Sooke, Skookumchuck and Skagit. Which province?

▷ *British Columbia*

Q Let's look for Makaroff, Manigotagan and De Salaberry.

▷ *Manitoba*

Q What lake am I?

Clue I. I cover about 350 square miles in Ontario! I'm shaped very much like a capital 'L' – each arm is about 40 miles long and 3 to 8 miles wide!

Clue II. I have thousands of islands in me! For that reason – the longest stretch of open water is only about a mile wide!

Clue III. The Canadian National Railway crosses me almost at my centre on trestle bridges that link some islands. And a river that shares my name carries overflow waters westward to the Lake of the Woods!

Clue IV. I'm right on the boundary between Ontario and Minnesota – about 125 miles north of Duluth!

▷ *Rainy Lake*

This is a multiple choice question. I'll give you a place name in a province of Canada and give you a choice of three directions by which you can locate it. You give me the correct direction. Here we go!

Q Is Barrie, Ontario a) west of Owen Sound, b) south of Chatham, or c) north of Guelph?

▷ *c) north of Guelph*

Q Is Red Deer, Alberta a) south of Edmonton, b) south of Calgary, or c) east of Medicine Hat?

▷ *a) south of Edmonton*

Q Is Kelowna, B.C. a) south of Vancouver, b) east of Kimberley, or c) north of Penticton?

▷ *c) north of Penticton*

Q Is Grand Falls, Newfoundland a) north of Twillingate, b) west of Bonavista, or c) east of St. John's?

▷ *b) west of Bonavista*

Q In Canada – all of these centres have something very much in common – and it's clearly in evidence – if you should happen to visit them! They are: Valcartier, Shearwater, Esquimalt and Borden!

▷ *Canadian Forces Bases*

Q During World War I I – the base at Esquimalt was the principal training establishment in Western Canada. Was it an Army, Navy or Air Force base?

▷ *Navy*

Q And CFB Borden – is in Ontario! It was established in 1916 and was capable of accommodating 30,000 soldiers in tents! One year later the RFC established a training station at Camp Borden! What was the RFC?

▷ *(The) Royal Flying Corps*

Q The Base at Shearwater has also been a Naval Training Centre over the years – but for a period during the last war – airmen were also trained there! In what province is Shearwater?

▷ *Nova Scotia*

Q Finally – CFB Valcartier! In relation to Quebec City – is Valcartier – North, West, East or South?

▷ *North (about 20 miles from Quebec City)*

Canadian Agriculture

Q It's grown in Nova Scotia, New Brunswick, southern Quebec, in much of Ontario and in the interior of British Columbia! It's Canada's most important commercial fruit! What is it?

▷ *(The) Apple*

38

Q In B.C. – the majority of the apples grown are found in a specific valley that shares its name with a lake and a river! What region is it?

▷ *The Okanagan Valley*

Q If the apple is the King of Canadian fruits – what fruit rates as the Prince? What fruit is Canada's second largest crop?

▷ *Peaches*

Q Again – British Columbia is a big producer! But B.C. shares the majority of this country's peach growing with another province – which one?

▷ *Ontario*

Q B.C. and Ontario – between them – grow and harvest a large percentage of Canada's overall crop of peaches! What percentage – is it 40% – 60% – 80%?

▷ *80%*

Canadiana

Q With which vital product do you associate these familiar names: Pembina, Redman, Regen, Selkirk and Fife?

▷ *Wheat (names of wheat strains!)*

Q Wheat is the world's leading grain crop and enjoys the distinction of being the oldest! As a matter of fact – wheat was cultivated as far back as 5,000 B.C. In what country was it grown at that time?

▷ *Egypt*

Q In Canada – in the 1840s – a farmer set about to develop European seedlings into a Spring wheat better suited to our climate. He was successful – and the strain still bears the man's name! What name?

▷ *Fife (his first name was David)*

Q That famous Spring wheat of Mr. Fife's was later developed into "Red" Fife and that strain was developed for a specific purpose! Why was it developed?

▷ *To resist rust (Rust is a parasitic fungus that attacks wheat!)*

If you've spent a lot of your spare time staring at atlases – you'll likely know the answers to these questions about some of Canada's waterways!

Q It's not called by that name now – but at one time one of our famous Canadian rivers was referred to as "The River of Disappointment" – called that by the man it disappointed. What is its name now?

▷ *The Mackenzie*

Q Sir Alexander Mackenzie called it "The River of Disappointment" during his exploration of the Western region in 1789! Why did he call it that?

▷ *Because it didn't lead to the Pacific Ocean!*

Q It didn't lead to the Pacific Ocean – but the Mackenzie does find its way to a certain Sea! What is its name?

▷ *The Beaufort (in the Western Arctic Ocean)*

Q Name this Canadian river – it's about 350 miles long – it rises in northeast British Columbia – it flows through Alberta's Wood Buffalo National Park and ends up in Great Slave Lake. What is it called?

▷ *The Hay River*

Quebec

Q What Canadian province has the largest area?

▷ *Quebec (594,860 sq. miles)*

Q What is Quebec's provincial flower?

▷ *White Garden Lily*

Q In what year was Quebec admitted to Confederation?

▷ *1867*

Q What is the population (to nearest million)?

▷ *6,023,000*

Q Geographically, Quebec is divided into three natural divisions. Identify one.

▷ *The Appalachian Region*
The St. Lawrence Lowlands
The Canadian Shield

Q From which part of the Appalachian region does about 85% of Canada's asbestos come?

▷ *The Eastern Townships*
(in the serpentine belt: Thetford Mines, Black Lake, Asbestos, etc.)

Q Which portion of the province of Quebec is included in the Appalachian Region?

▷ *The Gaspé Peninsula (Gaspesie) and the Eastern Townships*

Q Which of Canada's physiographic regions is the smallest, yet most productive and densely-populated?

▷ *The Great Lakes-St. Lawrence Lowlands Region*

Q What percentage of Canada's total population do the Lowlands contain?

▷ *About 60%*

Q Between which two geographical regions does the triangular area called the St. Lawrence Lowlands lie?

⟱ *The Canadian Shield (on the north) and the Appalachian Highlands (on the south)*

Q The low and flat uniformity of the Lowlands is broken by a group of eight widely-spaced conical peaks, extending from the Appalachian Highlands to which Canadian city?

⟱ *Montreal*

Q What is the group of widely-spaced hills, which are actually old volcanic plugs, today crowned by forests, and ringed by orchards, called?

⟱ *The Monteregian Hills*
(In the St. Lawrence River Valley, the eight peaks are called Royal, St. Bruno, Beloeil, Rougement, Yamaska, Shefford, Brome and Johnson.)

Energy Sources

It has been estimated that the world's oil reserves will supply enough oil for 36 more years at the current production levels. Other sources of energy must be found.

Q Another source of energy is nuclear power. Where was Canada's first experimental nuclear power station?

⟱ *Rolphton, Ontario (opened in 1962)*

Q Alberta's oil-saturated tar sands stretch for more than 100 miles along which river?

▷ *Athabasca River*

Q Which term describes a vast, V-shaped physiographic region around Hudson Bay?

▷ *Canadian Shield (covers 1,850,000 square miles)*

Q From which geologic age do the Canadian Shield's ancient igneous and metamorphic rocks date?

▷ *Precambrian Age (more than five million years ago)*

Q What is the highest point in the Canadian Shield in Ontario?

▷ *Mount Batchawana (2,100 ft.)*

Q What type of soil, especially characteristic of the Shield, is the most widespread in Canada?

▷ *Podzols/Spodosols*
(strongly acid, infertile humus, underlying a thin mat of leaves and decayed vegetation)

Q Which "axis" joins the Canadian Shield to the Adirondack Mountains of New York State in the vicinity of the Thousand Islands?

▷ *The Frontenac Axis*
(in the Rock or Clay Plains regional landform in southern Ontario)

The East

Q Which is the chief Atlantic ice-free port city in Canada?

▷ *Halifax (Nova Scotia)*

Q Nova Scotia is the Latin translation for New Scotland. Who was the individual responsible for naming Nova Scotia?

▷ *Sir William Alexander (later Earl of Stirling)*
(derived from the Latin charter by which New Scotland was granted to Alexander in 1621)

Q Halifax is the capital of Nova Scotia. Which Micmac Indian term, meaning "the chief harbour," originally referred to the Halifax location?

▷ *Chebucto (or Chebooktook)*

Q Which long, straight, fertile valley is the great apple region of Nova Scotia?

▷ *Annapolis Valley*

Q How is Cape Breton connected to the mainland?

▷ *By the Canso Causeway (from Sydney to Halifax, a distance of 263 miles)*

Canadian Waters

Q Which is the largest group of fresh-water lakes in the world?

▷ *The Great Lakes*

Q From which two provinces does the Gulf of Mexico drain waters?

▷ *Alberta and Saskatchewan*

Q The St. Lawrence Seaway allows ocean freighters of 27-foot draught to enter the Great Lakes. When was the Seaway completed?

▷ *1959 (It opened officially in June, 1959.)*

Q Can you name two of the six main basins of watersheds draining Canada's rivers?

▷ *a) Pacific Coast Basin*
  b) Arctic Basin
  c) Hudson Bay Basin
  d) Great Lake-St. Lawrence Basin
  e) Atlantic Coast Basin
  f) Gulf of Mexico Basin

Q There are seven locks in the St. Lawrence Seaway, between Montreal and Lake Ontario. How many of these locks are within Canadian waters?

▷ *Five Locks (operated and maintained by the St. Lawrence Seaway Authority)*

Canadian Waterways

Rivers and lakes were once an essential part of our transportation system, and not that long ago, either. Although water travel has fallen into disuse recently, I hope you still know some of our major water paths and sources.

Q Which river flows 410 miles into Hudson Bay from Lake Winnipeg?

▷ *Nelson River*
(1,600 miles between the Rocky Mountains and the Bow River)

Q Which lake, located in the Northwest Territories, is the fourth largest lake on the North American continent?

▷ *Great Bear Lake (12,275 sq. miles)*

Q What is the name of Canada's longest river system, which flows into the Arctic Ocean?

▷ *Mackenzie (River System)*
(2,635 miles from the Finlay River source in B.C.)

Q Including its most remote tributary, the Finlay River, what 1,195-mile river flows into the Mackenzie River via Slave River?

▷ *Peace River*

Q What river flows about 1,200 miles ultimately into the Pacific Ocean in the United States?

⇨ *Columbia River (459 miles are in Canada)*

Natural Physical Features

Q In which province is the Missouri Coteau located?

⇨ *Saskatchewan*
(it separates the 2nd from the 3rd prairie level)

Q In which province is the Liard Plain located?

⇨ *(Northern) British Columbia*

Q In which province is the Ungava Trough located?

⇨ *Quebec (important ore deposit area)*

Q In which province is the Tantramar Marsh to be found?

⇨ *New Brunswick (along the banks of the Tantramar River)*

Q In which province is the Frontenac Axis located?

⇨ *Ontario (in the Thousand Islands area)*

Unique Canadian Place Names

Canada is a nation dotted with a tremendous variety of unique place names. In what provinces can you find places with names like this?

Q Czar?

▷ *Alberta*

Q False Girdle?

▷ *Newfoundland*

Q Hoochekoo Creek?

▷ *Yukon Territory*

Q Bay of God's Mercy?

▷ *Northwest Territories*

Q Peep-O-Day Creek?

▷ *British Columbia*

Q Péribonca River? (pronounced pair-ih-bonk-ah)

▷ *Quebec*

Q Push-And-Be-Damned-Rapids?

New Brunswick

Q Slingdung Brook?

New Brunswick

The North

Q What is the capital of the Yukon Territories?

Whitehorse

Q What happened in the Yukon of importance in 1896?

Gold was discovered.

Q What is the highest point in the Yukon?

Mount Logan

Q What is the title of the senior officer of government?

Commissioner

Q What type of glacial moraine is formed when two lateral moraines meet on a piedmont glacier?

Medial moraine

Q Many of the Canadian Arctic coastal fiords are immense. Which Baffin Island fiord is the longest in Canada and the world?

⟩ *Admiralty Inlet*
(160 miles, combined with Easter Sound, 8 miles, and Berlinguet Inlet, 42 miles, for a total of 210 miles)

Q In geological terminology, what do the words, rind, pancake, young, winter and brash refer to?

⟩ *Types of ice (referring to the stages of ice formation on the surface of the sea)*

One of the greatest factors in the development of the Northern Territories has been the exploration for valuable minerals. In 1896, Dawson City had its gold. In 1913, Mayo had its lead and silver deposits. In the years given, what were the following sites noted for:

Q Great Bear Lake, in 1930?

⟩ *Uranium (located in Northwest Territories)*

Q United Keno Hill Mines, in 1950?

⟩ *Silver/lead/zinc (located in Yukon Territory)*

Q Dawson, Y.T., in 1968?

⟩ *Asbestos*

Q Norman Wells, N.W.T., in 1920?

⟩ *Oil*

Out West

Q What is the province of Manitoba's official floral emblem?

▷ *The Prairie Crocus*

Q In what year was the Winnipeg Grain Exchange established?

▷ *1887 (then called the Winnipeg and Produce Exchange)*

Q What is the Indian meaning of the word "Manitoba"?

▷ *Strait of the Manitu, or Spirit*

Q James Woodsworth was a founder of the CCF party. What do the letters CCF mean?

▷ *Co-operative Commonwealth Federation*

Q Against which standard is the quality of all bread wheats measured in Canada?

▷ *Number One Hard Red Spring Wheat – known throughout the world as "Manitobas"*

Traditionally, eastern Canada has led in economic and cultural developments for this country. However, the recent importance placed upon the resources of the Prairie Provinces may soon shift the centre of Canada's evolution.

Q Which geologic anomaly was once described by the western prairie explorer, Captain John Palliser, as "a perfect oasis in the desert we have travelled"?

▷ *The Cypress Hills (the name appears on the Palliser map of 1865)*

Q Which type of wheat is the result of a cross between Hard Red Calcutta and Red Fife wheats?

▷ *Marquis Wheat*

Q For which province is the increasingly-hard-to-find Prairie Lily the floral emblem?

▷ *Saskatchewan*

National Preserves

These questions are for the campers in the crowd. Tell me the province in which these National Parks are located:

Q In which province is Cape Breton Highlands National Park?

▷ *Nova Scotia*

Q Where are the alpine meadows of Mount Revelstoke National Park located?

▷ *British Columbia*

Q In which province is Point Pelee National Park located?

⬭ *Ontario*

Q In which province is Banff National Park located?

⬭ *Alberta*

Q In which province is Prince Albert Park with its excellent streams for canoeing?

⬭ *Saskatchewan*

Cities and Towns

In which provinces are these cities located?

Q Sarnia?

⬭ *Ontario*

Q Kelowna?

⬭ *British Columbia*

Q Portage la Prairie?

⬭ *Manitoba*

Q Medicine Hat?

> *Alberta*

Q Hull?

> *Quebec*

Q Wabana?

> *Newfoundland*

Q Glace Bay?

> *Nova Scotia*

Q Montague?

> *Prince Edward Island*

Q Oromocto?

> *New Brunswick*

Q Moose Jaw?

> *Saskatchewan*

Q Which provincial capital city was once known as Fort Camosun?

> *Victoria, B.C.*

Q Which city is connected to the provincial capital by the Angus L. Macdonald Bridge?

▷ *Dartmouth (Nova Scotia)*

Q What city, also the name of a federal constituency, is located on the south bank of the Saguenay River?

▷ *Chicoutimi (Quebec)*

Q Which northern Saskatchewan city has the same name as a National Park in that province?

▷ *Prince Albert*

Q Which harbour city, once the capital of the old province of Cape Breton, is today an important centre of coal-mining and the steel industry?

▷ *Sydney*

Q Which important business centre, situated across the Red River from the provincial capital city, is also the distinctive home of French and Catholic culture in the province?

▷ *St. Boniface (Manitoba)*

Q What Atlantic province city, located on a river that flows into the Gulf of St. Lawrence, is the site of a large, British paper mill?

▷ *Corner Brook (Nfld.)*
(site of Bowater's Newfoundland Pulp and Paper Mills Ltd.)

Down East

Q What was the first city to be incorporated in Canada?

> *Saint John*
> *(developed in 1783 with the arrival of the United Empire*
> *Loyalists and incorporated in 1785)*

Q What is the "Bore"?

> *A tidal wave (it comes up the Petitcodiac River, twice in every*
> *24 hours)*

Q Geophysically, New Brunswick belongs to the region known
as what?

> *The Acadian Highland*

Q Which city was known, until 1885, as the "Bend of the
Petitcodiac"?

> *Moncton*
> *(named after Robert Moncton, commander of the British*
> *force that, in 1755, captured Fort Beauséjour, 40 miles away)*

P.E.I.

Q Canada's smallest province is called P.E.I. What does P.E.I.
stand for?

> *Prince Edward Island*

Q Who was Prince Edward?

⟣ *Duke of Kent, father of Queen Victoria*

Q Before 1800, what did the French originally call Prince Edward Island?

⟣ *Isle St. Jean/St. John's Island*

Q Which provincial town is situated on Hillsborough Bay?

⟣ *Charlottetown (Prince Edward Island)*
(on a sheltered arm of Northhumberland Strait)

Q How many political counties is the Island divided into?

⟣ *Three (Prince, Queen's and King's)*

Q A car ferry service, operated by the CN, crosses the Northumberland Strait between which two towns?

⟣ *Tormentine (New Brunswick) and Borden (Prince Edward Island)*

Mountains

Do you know your mountains?

Q What is the highest peak in the Rocky Mountain division?

⟣ *Mt. Robson (12,972 ft.)*

Q
On a physiographic map of Canada, indicating the seven main regions, what is the westernmost, mountainous region called?

▷ *The Western Cordilleras*

Q
What is the highest peak in the Cariboo Mountains of the Interior Ranges?

▷ *Mt. Sir Wilfrid Laurier (11,750 ft.)*

Q
What is the highest peak in the adjacent Selkirk Mountains?

▷ *Mt. Sir Sandford (11,590 ft.)*

Q
What is the highest alpine peak of the Coastal Mountain Ranges of British Columbia?

▷ *Mt. Waddington (13,260 ft.)*

Q
What is British Columbia's highest mountain peak?

▷ *Mt. Fairweather (15,300 ft.) (in the St. Elias chain)*

General Geographical Facts

Q
Canada is the second largest country in the world – 3.8 million square miles in area. Which is the third largest country?

▷ *People's Republic of China (with territories)*
(area under control: 3,691,502 sq. miles)

Q What is the Quebec Island at the eastern tip of the Gaspé Peninsula?

▷ *Bonaventure Island*

Q Which two Canadian provinces do not border on salt water?

▷ *Alberta & Saskatchewan*

Q What is the name of the passage between the B.C. mainland and the Queen Charlotte Islands?

▷ *Hecate Strait*
(named after one of Capt. G.H. Richard's ships when he surveyed the B.C. coast)

Q Under what name, in 1970, were the Ontario cities of Port Arthur and Fort William and their surrounding municipalities amalgamated?

▷ *Thunder Bay*

Q Which Canadian province in the Atlantic Region has a town called Christmas Island?

▷ *Nova Scotia*

Q Which country owns Banks, Bathurst, and the fifth largest island in the world, Baffin Island?

▷ *Canada*

Q In 1897, what was the largest city west of Winnipeg?

⇨ *Dawson City (Yukon Territory)*
(In 1898 it had a population of 25,000 due to the gold rush)

Q What is the world's most northern settlement?

⇨ *Alert, Ellesmere Island, (N.W.T.) (operated jointly by Canada and the U.S.)*

Q What is the world's largest freshwater lake?

⇨ *Lake Superior (31,800 sq. miles)*

Q Which strait separating Greenland from Baffin Island joins Baffin Bay with the Labrador Sea in North America?

⇨ *Davis Strait*

Q Which U.S. supertanker made experimental voyages through the Northwest Passage in 1969 and 1970?

⇨ *The U.S.S. "Manhattan"*

Q On which island is Cape Columbia, Canada's most northerly point?

⇨ *Ellesmere Island*
(it lies closer to the North Pole than any other land in the world except the northern tip of Greenland)

Q Which island is Canada's most southerly point?

⇨ *Middle Island (south of Pelee Island in Lake Erie)*

More about Ontario:

Mining ranks as one of Ontario's most important industries.

Q In what year did the Constitutional Act divide Quebec into Upper and Lower Canada?

▷ *1791*
(The Ottawa River was used as the dividing line)

Q Until 1878, what was the Canadian National Exhibition, held in an Ontario city, called?

▷ *The Toronto Exhibition (first held in 1846)*

Q What are two of the four major land regions into which Ontario is divided geophysically?

▷ *Hudson Bay Lowland*
The Canadian Shield
The Lower Great Lakes Lowlands
St. Lawrence Lowlands

Names and Places

Q What city am I?

Clue I. I am a North American harbor city, first discovered by Europeans in 1497.

Clue I I. I am situated 565 miles by rail from Port aux Basques.

Clue III. My name originated from a feast in the Anglican and Roman Catholic Churches, celebrated on June 24th, my founding date.

Clue IV. My fine, landlocked harbor, my piers and drydock, make me a centre of the fishing and shipping industries.

▷ *St. John's, Newfoundland*

Q If you were in "the city of the Foothills," where would you be?

▷ *Calgary*

How about these?

Q "The Gateway to the Dominion"?

▷ *Halifax*

Q "The Bend, the Hub of the Maritimes"?

▷ *Moncton*

Q "The Gibraltar of North America"?

▷ *Quebec*

Q "The City of Gardens"?

▷ *Victoria*

Q "The Peg"?

▷ *Winnipeg*

Q "Canada's Golden Gateway," "Gastown," "Gateway to the Orient"?

▷ *Vancouver*

Q "The Cradle of Confederation"?

▷ *Charlottetown*

Q "The Forest City"?

▷ *London, Ontario*

Q "Gateway to the North"?

▷ *Edmonton*

Q "The Telephone City"?

▷ *Brantford*

Q What prairie city was once known as "Pile of Bones"?

▷ *Regina. . . . That's right. Before settlers started arriving in the area, this region was a popular place for the Indians to hunt buffalo. The great herds were run into stockades called "pounds," set up along the Wascana creek. Once forced into the pounds they were killed by the Indians with rifles and arrows. When settlers arrived they found immense bone piles left over from the seasonal hunts.*

64

Q Well, if it was called "Pile of Bones," why was the name changed to Regina?

▷ *In 1882, when the first train arrived at "Pile of Bones," the settlement needed a name for the station and "Pile of Bones" just wasn't suitable – it certainly wasn't a name that would attract settlers. So someone thought of Regina, the Latin word for Queen, in honour of Queen Victoria. But the Wascana creek is still there to remind folks of their past. Wascana is the Cree Indian word for "Pile of Bones."*

The Things People Say about Canadian Cities.

Q What do you think of Regina, Sir John A. Macdonald?

▷ *"If you had a little more wood and a little more water, and here and there a hill, I think the prospect would be improved." (spoken on his first trip across the country by CPR in 1886)*

Q How did you think up the name of "Saskatoon," Mr. John N. Lake (he led the party of the Temperance Colonization Co. to the site of the modern city on August 20, 1882)?

▷ *"We thought of Minnetonka for a name, but found some Saskatoon berries and that settled it."*

Q Do you have anything to say about Quebec City, Mr. Thomas Haliburton?

▷ *"The French thought building a fortress was colonization, and the English that blowing it up was the right way to settle the country." (Nature and Human Nature, 1855)*

And Mark Twain was singularly impressed with Montreal: *"This is the first time I was ever in a city where you couldn't throw a brick without breaking a church window." (speech in Montreal, Dec. 5, 1881)*

Canadian Sport

Q Did a Canadian ever win the world's heavyweight championship?

▷ *Yes. Tommy Burns, born near Hanover, Ontario on June 7, 1881, was the only Canadian ever to win the heavyweight championship. He didn't enter the ring until 1900, when, in Detroit, he stood in for a boxer who failed to show up. But it was not until 1906 that he won the world's championship. He held the title for more than 2 years, defeating all comers in the U.S., Britain, Ireland, France and Australia, finally losing to Jack Johnson of the U.S. in Sydney, Australia in 1908. Tommy Burns didn't give up easily; police had to stop that fight in the 14th round! Burns quit the ring for 4 years and despite a comeback and some victories, he never again enjoyed fame as a boxer. When he finally left the ring, he operated a hotel in England, then a speakeasy in New York. He ended his days as an evangelist in Vancouver, where he died in 1955.*

With which sport are the following associated:

Q George Hayes, Bill Chadwick, Frank Udvari and Matt Pavelich?

▷ *Professional ice hockey (they are referees and linesmen)*

Q Anne Jardin, Bruce Robertson, Wendy Cook, Bruce Rogers and Patti Stenhouse?

▷ *Swimming*

Q Peter Kirby, Doug Lyon, Gary Cowan, Dan Halldorson, Ben Kern and Wilf Homeniuk?

⟐ *Golf*

Q Donald Jackson, Jay Humphrey and Wendy Griner?

⟐ *Figure Skating*
(They are all former Canadian national figure skating champions)

Q Dale Power, Jane O'Hara, David Brown and Don McCormick?

⟐ *Tennis*

Q Who was "Tom Longboat," the man with the six-foot-six stride?

⟐ *Tom Longboat, a great Canadian runner, was born on the Six Nations reserve near Brantford, Ontario. In 1907, at the age of 20, he was chosen by the Toronto YMCA to run in the classic 25-mile Boston Marathon. Along a crowd-packed route, he beat 125 competitors to establish a record that lasted a number of years.*

Q Two teams are involved and it's played on a field! It's also a rough game! Canada's national game. It's called?

⟐ *Lacrosse*

Q The Canadian Lacrosse Association founded in Winnipeg in 1925 makes awards each year to the Junior and Senior Amateur Champions! The Silver Trophy goes to the Junior Amateur Champions – and it's named for the Governor General who donated it! What is the trophy called?

▷ *The Minto Cup*

Q The solid gold trophy is presented to the Senior Champions each year – what name does it bear?

▷ *Mann!*

Q Named after Sir Donald Mann! What was Sir Donald's claim to fame – in which particular field did he excel?

▷ *Railroad building!*
(he built the Canadian Northern Railway!)

Q Who am I?

Clue I. I was born in Winnipeg in 1929. Although as fate would have it – my name became more closely associated with other cities! Including Toronto, Los Angeles and Detroit!

Clue II. I was closely associated as well with the cities of Boston and New York – they were part of my outstanding 20-year career as a hockey player!

Clue III. I played more games and more seasons and recorded more shut-outs than any other goal keeper in NHL history!

70

Clue IV. During my spectacular goal-tending years I was credited with at least 100 shut-outs! I was only 41 when I died in 1970!

▷ *Terry Sawchuck!*

NHL Hockey

Q In which Canadian city is the NHL Hockey Hall of Fame?

▷ *Toronto (Ontario)*
(officially opened August 26, 1961, by then Prime Minister Diefenbaker)

Q What basic qualification must a person meet in order to be considered for membership in the Hockey Hall of Fame?

▷ *"Any person who is or has been distinguished as a player, executive, or as a referee shall be eligible for election."*
(chosen on the basis of playing ability, integrity, character and their contribution to their team and the game in general)

Q Although the Stanley Cup has been sought for three-quarters of a century, relatively few players have made it to the Hall of Fame. Is the number 97, 121 or 152?

▷ *152 (152 players, 56 builders, and 8 referees)*

Q On November 2nd, 1959, in New York, a "first" in NHL history occurred. This "first" was later placed in the Hall of Fame. What was it?

▷ *Jacques Plante's face mask*

Q The fastest three pucks ever scored in NHL history are also placed in the Hockey Hall of Fame. In seconds, how fast were those pucks?

▷ *21 seconds*

Q Which trophy is given to the leading scorer?

▷ *The Art Ross Trophy*
(an annual award "to the player who leads the league in scoring points at the end of the regular season"; Arthur Howie Ross presented the trophy to the NHL in 1947)

Q The James Norris Memorial Trophy is given to which position?

▷ *Best defenseman*
(an annual award "to the defense player who demonstrates throughout the season the greatest all-around ability in that position")

Q Which trophy is given for best rookie?

▷ *The Calder Trophy*
(An annual award "to the player selected as the most proficient in his first year of competition in the NHL". Presented originally in 1936-7, the new trophy was presented by the NHL after Frank Calder's death in 1943.)

The Stanley Cup was placed in competition in 1893, just 18 years after the first formalized hockey rules were created.

Q Which NHL coach saw his team win more Stanley Cup competitions than any other coach?

▷ *Hector (Toe) Blake*

Q Can you identify the team that Toe Blake coached to eight Stanley Cup victories?

▷ *The Montreal Canadiens*
(Toe Blake: coach of the Canadiens since 1955)

Q The Montreal Canadiens have won 17 Stanley Cup victories since the NHL was formed in 1917. Prior to the formation of the league, in what year was their first Stanley Cup victory?

▷ *1916*

Q The longest recorded hockey game was 2 hours, 56 minutes and 30 seconds. It took 6 periods of overtime hockey before the Detroit Red Wings could bring down which team?

▷ *The Montreal Maroons (in 1936)*
(the 1934–35 Stanley Cup winners, the Maroons retired from the NHL in 1938. The final score was Detroit 1 - Montreal 0)

Which National Hockey League team plays its home games in:

Q The Pacific Coliseum?

▷ *Vancouver Canucks*

Q Maple Leaf Gardens?

  ▷ *Toronto Maple Leafs*

Q Montreal Forum?

  ▷ *Montreal Canadiens*

With the continuing expansion of the National Hockey League, a Four-Division format has been devised to streamline the competition for playoff positions. I'll name the hockey team. You tell me to which Division that team belongs.

Q The California Seals?

  ▷ *The (Weston) Adams Division*

Q The Philadelphia Flyers?

  ▷ *The (Lester) Patrick Division*

Q The Vancouver Canucks?

  ▷ *The (Conn) Smythe Division*

Q The New York Islanders?

  ▷ *The (Lester) Patrick Division*

The first ice hockey activity in North America was in 1855. Since then, the rules of the game have been expanded and revised, as well as hockey terminology.

Q What do the initials "P.I.M." stand for?

▷ *Penalties in minutes*

Q Which hockey term refers to "checking of an opponent by a forward, in that forward's own defensive zone"?

▷ *Back Checking*

Q What is a "player who specializes in playing when his team is short-handed," commonly called?

▷ *Penalty Killer*

Q Which hockey term refers to "a five-minute penalty, usually for fighting, or intent to injure"?

▷ *Major penalty*

Football

The argument has been going on for a long time about which is better – Canadian or American-style football. Let's look at some of the rule differences between the two games.

Q The size of the field is an obvious difference when comparing the two games. Which has the larger field?

▷ *Canada*
  (the Canadian field is 100 metres x 60 metres; the American field 91 metres long x 49 metres wide)

Q The number of men on the field is one of the most obvious differences between the two games. In the Canadian game, there are 12 men on the field at any one time for each team. In American football, how many men may one team have on the field?

▷ *Eleven*

Q No time-outs are permitted in Canadian football, except when the clock stops for changes, or for the wishes of the referee. In American football, each team is permitted time-outs of 90-second durations. What is the maximum number of time-outs allowed for each team in a game?

▷ *Six (three in each half)*

Q At the beginning of each half, the ball is kicked off from the 45-yard line in Canada. Where do the Americans kick the ball off from?

▷ *The 40-yard line*

Name the home stadium of the following CFL teams.

Q Ottawa?

▷ *Lansdowne Park*

Q Saskatchewan?

▷ *Taylor Field*

Q Montreal?

▷ *Olympic Stadium*

Q British Columbia?

▷ *Empire Stadium*

Q Toronto?

▷ *Exhibition Stadium*

Q Edmonton?

▷ *Clarke Stadium*

Q Hamilton?

▷ *Ivor Wynne Stadium*

Q Calgary?

 McMahon Stadium

Q Winnipeg?

Winnipeg Stadium

Canadian sports are divided into approximately 60 associations. Most of these are members of national associations. I'll give you their initials; you tell me what they stand for.

Q S.F.C.?

Sports Federation of Canada
(formerly the C.A.S.F. – Canadian Amateur Sports Federation)

Q C.A.H.P.E.R.?

Canadian Association for Health, Physical Education &
Recreation

Q C.O.A.?

Canadian Olympic Association
(Head Office and Secretariat in Montreal)

Q C.I.A.U.?

Canadian Intercollegiate Athletic Union

78

Q What is the recently-formed association which concentrates on developing the science and art of coaching – initials C.A.A.?

▷ *Coaching Association of Canada*
(based in Vanier, Ontario – which is just east of Ottawa)

Q In the 1972 Munich Olympics, Canadians David Miller, John Ekels and Paul Côté jointly won a bronze medal for which event?

▷ *Yacht Racing (Solings category)*

Q The Olympic Gold Medal is the highest award given in the Olympic Games. Which country has won more Olympic Gold Medals for ice hockey than any other country?

▷ *Canada (for a total of 6 Gold Medals)*

Q At the 1928 games in Amsterdam, which Canadian won the Olympic Gold Medals for his achievements in running the 100 metres and 200 metres competitions?

▷ *Percy Williams (times of 10.8 and 21.8 respectively)*
(the only Canadian ever to win both titles)

Q Who was the first player in the NHL to attempt a "penalty shot?"

▷ *(William Scott) "Scotty" Bowman*
(the penalty shot was introduced in NHL rules in the 1934-35 season)

Who's Who in Sports

Q With which sport do we associate Nancy Greene Rains?

⇨ *Skiing (this British Columbia skier won an Olympic Gold Medal at Grenoble in 1968)*

What about these sports stars:

Q Bill Bynum?

⇨ *Football*

Q Don Baylor?

⇨ *Baseball*

Q Tom Weiskopf?

⇨ *Golf*

Q Jim Elder?

⇨ *Horseback riding*

Q Name the Edmonton Eskimos star who had the nickname "Old Spaghetti Legs".

⇨ *Jackie Parker (came to Edmonton in 1954; stayed until 1962; to Toronto in 1963; played in 4 Grey Cup games for Edmonton: 2 as halfback; 2 as quarterback)*

Q Name the winner of Canada's first Olympic Gold Medal for figure skating?

⇨ *Barbara Ann Scott (in 1948) (She was born in Ottawa, in 1928.)*

Q When they were playing for the Boston hockey club, Bobby Bauer, "Milt" Schmidt and Woody Dumart were collectively known by what name?

⇨ *The "Kraut" Line (the three played together as a "Bruins" line in the late 1940s and early 1950s)*

Q He has earned over $10 million . . . as much as $2 million in a single season – quite an achievement for a country boy with a grade 5 education. Who is this man, one of Canada's richest athletes?

⇨ *Hervé Filion*

Q In what sport is he engaged? He has driven over 5,000 winners, more than any other North American.

⇨ *Horse racing (trots)*

Q What is the conveyance Filion sits on during the race?

⇨ *Sulky*

Q Filion has won numerous honours – he was the first French Canadian to be included in Canada's special tribute to sports heroes which is called?

⇨ *Canada's Sports Hall of Fame*

Q Who was the "World's Strongest Man"?

▷ *Louis Cyr (1863–1912), a champion weight-lifter and, at one point, a star attraction of the Ringling Brothers and Barnum & Bailey circuses. He is reported to have weighed 18 pounds at birth: at the peak of his career, he tipped the scales at 365 pounds although he was only 5 ft. 10 1/2 in. tall!*

Cyr began his career as a Montreal policeman. In the very unusual arrest which made him famous, he picked up three toughs and carried them several city blocks back to the station, one under each arm and a third in an arm-grip in front of him. When news of his feat reached the New York newspapers, he was hired as circus strong man for "The Greatest Show on Earth"! His most famous stunt was lifting a heavily loaded platform with his shoulders. Once, in Montreal, he mystified the crowd by lifting 4,562 pounds!

Q Who am I?

Clue I. I grew up in Kirkland Lake, Ontario and began to take an interest in skating at the age of 7. At 15 I captured the Canadian Junior Championship.

Clue II. About this time I met Ellen Burka of Toronto, mother and coach of Petra Burka, 1965 winner of the women's world championship. She agreed to take me on as a pupil.

Clue III. Some people have difficulty deciding whether I am a champion figure skater who paints or a promising painter who does figure skating.

Clue IV. I just made a smash hit on Broadway with my new and different ice show.

▷ *Toller Cranston*

82

History

Canada is a Great Country!

Let's look for some "greats" within the great land!

Q Just a few years prior to Confederation, a Union Government of the Province of Canada was formed! It was labelled "The Great Coalition" because it joined the Conservatives and the Clear Grits! The Conservatives were led by Macdonald and Cartier – but who was the head of the Grits?

▷ *George Brown*

Q The far North of Canada was once described as "The Great White Land" by a man who knew a great deal about that part of the world. He mentioned "The Great White Land" in a novel he wrote in 1910 called *The Trail of '98*! The writer was a Canadian – what was his name?

▷ *Robert Service*

Q If you were miles from home – and you met a stranger – and you were pleased to know that he was also from "The Great Island" – where in Canada did you both come from?

▷ *Newfoundland*

Q It's still with us today – but what early organization in Canada was referred to as "The Great Company"?

▷ *The Hudson's Bay Co.*

Q We're all familiar with Great Bear Lake, Great Slave Lake, Great Fall, and the Great Lakes – but do you remember the Great Fish River? It's about 600 miles long. It's also called the Back River! Where in Canada does it flow?

▷ *Mackenzie District/Northwest Territories!*

The Capital

Q Who chose Ottawa as Canada's capital?

▷ *Queen Victoria*

Q What buildings, erected in the 1860s, dominate the city's core?

▷ *(Canada's) Parliament buildings*

Q The Parliament buildings are actually a group of three buildings: the Centre Block, East Block and West Block. The original Centre Block was built in a Gothic style. Who was its chief designer?

▷ *Thomas Fuller (Augustus Laver was his associate architect)*

Q Which dignitary laid the cornerstone for the Centre Block on September 1st, 1860?

⇨ *The Prince of Wales (who later became Edward VII)*

Q What famous event took place at the Parliament buildings on the night of February 3rd, 1916?

⇨ *Fire swept the Centre Block*
(It destroyed most of the structure except for the Library, which was saved by the iron doors in the communicating corridor.)

Q The fire began in the newspaper reading room and spread quickly through the dry wooden corridors. Seven people lost their lives in the fire. How many of the seven were Members of Parliament?

⇨ *One*
(He was Bowman K. Law, the member for Yarmouth, N.S. The others were visitors and employees.)

Q The most dramatic moment came at midnight. It is said that spectators gasped in amazement because of a strange coincidence. What was it?

⇨ *The huge clock on the tall tower crashed into flames just as the bell sounded the final stroke of twelve!!*

Q That same bell is the only part of the old building that can still be seen on Parliament Hill. It's on the grounds next to one of the buildings that make up the present complex. Outside what particular building is the bell located?

▷ *The Library*

Q The commanding feature of the new Centre Block was the Peace Tower. In 1919, another Prince of Wales laid the cornerstone for the tower. Is the Peace Tower closer to 300 ft. high, 400 ft. high or 500 ft. high?

▷ *300 ft. high (It contains a Memorial Chamber with an Altar of Sacrifice. On the altar are the Books of Remembrance in which are inscribed the names of Canadians who died in active service in the two World Wars.)*

Q The new buildings were not completed until the impressive Tower was erected. In what year in the 20s was that job completed?

▷ *1927 (designed by John Pearson)*

Q Is the beaver or the maple leaf Canada's official national emblem?

▷ *Canada had no official national emblem, although the maple leaf and the beaver were both considered as such by Canadians, until the Proclamation of the Canadian National Flag on Feb. 15, 1965, confirmed the maple leaf as Canada's emblem. (The beaver was the earliest symbol of Canada, because of the fur trade. The maple leaf started to gain in popularity around 1800.)*

Q What is the name of the Arctic owl souvenir – made of sealskin – that has become the symbol of the Canadian North?

▷ *Ookpik!*
The very first Ookpik doll was made by an Eskimo woman named Jeannie Snowball, at Fort Chimo, Quebec. That first Ookpik was a great success outside of Canada, many miles from the place where it was made. It was put on display at a large United States Trade Fair in Philadelphia in 1963. Because of its enthusiastic foreign reception Ookpik was then manufactured commercially on a large scale. When Mrs. Snowball named Ookpik – she couldn't have chosen a better Eskimo word! "Ookpik" means "Happy Little Arctic Owl."

Q Where does the Canadian motto "A Mari Usque ad Mare" come from and what does it mean?

▷ *Our national motto is a Latin phrase meaning "from sea to sea." It is an exact translation from the Latin, verse 8 of the 72nd Psalm: "He shall have dominion also from sea to sea, and from the river unto the ends of the earth."*

Q What is a "sod house?"

▷ *During settlement of the Canadian Prairies, the "sod house" or "brown front" was very popular. There were few raw materials on the empty prairie, and a good sod house could be made for a few dollars. Thousands were built on the Prairies between 1900 and 1910. The walls and roof of most of the houses were of sod. To build a sod house, furrows were plowed 12 or 14 inches apart in a grassy slough bottom, where the roots of the grasses held the sod together. The sod cuttings were laid much like bricks, row on row, then levelled off with a sharp spade. Poplar poles supported the roof, which often continued to grow, producing wild flowers throughout the summer. The covering of half an acre or 50 tons of sod, went into a good-sized sod house (say 30 ft. long). The building was expected to last 20 years. Most have long since vanished from the prairie, but some sod houses have survived to this day.*

Q What were the "silk trains" of Canadian history?

▷ *Faster than the fastest passenger trains, the "silk trains" raced across Canada from Vancouver to the market cities of eastern Canada and the United States. Their cargo, the beautiful silks of the Orient, was sealed in special containers to protect them from moisture and thieves. The only passengers on these trains were the armed men who guarded the silk. Daily changes in market prices made speed very important. In addition, the cargos were valuable, sometimes worth up to $6,000,000. The trains had priority over everything. Once the late King, George VI, then Duke of York, was shunted to a siding to let the silk train through!*

Q What was the Underground Railroad?

▷ *It was neither underground nor was it a railroad. Rather, it was routes which were used by fugitive slaves to reach Canada. The "stations" were homes of Abolitionists, who fed the fleeing slaves when they arrived and transported them under cover of darkness to the next station. It is estimated that 25,000 slaves obtained their freedom before the Civil War via the "Underground Railroad."*

Heroics and Disasters

Q Which Norse explorer is believed to have discovered North America almost 500 years before Christopher Columbus?

▷ *Leif "The Lucky" Ericson*
(during his expedition in the year 1000, he sailed along the Newfoundland coast to the North American mainland which he named "Vinland")

Q Who was "Dollard des Ormeaux" or "Adam Dollard"?

▷ *In 1660, Adam Dollard was a 25-year-old commander of the fort of Ville-Marie (now part of the city of Montreal). He heard that the Iroquois were planning to attack the city. With 16 men, he left to cut them off at the Long Sault. On the way, the French were joined by 44 Hurons and 4 Algonquins. At the Long Sault, they were attacked by 300 Iroquois, and within a few days, 500 more joined them. His Indian supporters deserted him, but Dollard held out for another ten days. Overwhelmed, finally, all the surviving 5 French were put to death.*

Q Has there ever been a political assassination in Canada?

▷ *Yes*
D'Arcy McGee, one of the Fathers of Confederation, on entering his house on Sparks Street, Ottawa, was shot in the head on April 7, 1868. The Fenians, agitating for Irish independence, were immediately suspected, as McGee had been strongly outspoken against them. No conspiracy was ever proven, but a young Irish tailor, Patrick James Whelan, was accused and hanged in 1869. (It was, incidentally, one of the most gruesome executions in Canadian history. The amateur hangman failed to make the drop long enough to break the condemned man's neck and he strangled as thousands watched.)

Q What was the Frank Slide?

⇨ *The Frank Slide was Canada's worst landslide. At 4:10 A.M., April 29, 1903, a gigantic wedge of limestone, approx. 2,000 feet high, 3,000 feet wide and 500 feet thick crashed down from neighboring Turtle Mountain and destroyed part of the town of Frank, Alberta. Some ninety million tons swept over two miles of the valley, taking about 100 lives, burying numerous homes, the whole mining plant, railway tracks and 3,200 acres of fertile land to a depth of 100 feet. All this occurred in only 100 seconds! The main business area was, happily, not crushed, or many more lives might have been lost.*

Q In November, 1956, one of this country's worst mining disasters struck what maritime town?

⇨ *Springhill, Nova Scotia (As a result of an explosion 112 miners were entombed and 39 died.)*

Contemporary Canadian History

I'll name the events – you name the year!

Q On January 17th during this year Mrs. Pauline McGibbon became the first woman ever to be appointed to a vice-regal post in Canada – she became the Lieutenant-Governor of Ontario. The last member of the Group of Seven painters, A.Y. Jackson died on April 5th of this year and the first Indian to be appointed a Lieutenant-Governor in this country – Ralph Steinhauer – took office in Alberta! It was the 70s!

⇨ *1974*

Q
This was the year Kingston, Ontario celebrated its 300th birthday, and in this year, on January 4th – a former Premier of Ontario died – he was George Drew. Also in this year, the Anik communications satellite began delivering live TV programmes to Arctic Canadians! In the 70s!

▷ *1973*

Q
During this year, two outstanding painters died – Arthur Lismer on March 23rd and Frederick Varley on September 10th. It was also the year that the oil tanker "Manhattan" became the first commercial ship to sail through the Northwest Passage! In the 60s!

▷ *1969*

Q
This year – a Royal Commission was appointed on the 5th of February to "investigate Russian espionage in Canada" and the "Bluenose" sank off the island of Haiti! And – Mackenzie King established a record for longevity as this country's prime minister! It was in the 1940s. Which year?

▷ *1946*

Canadian Political History

Q
Which British report followed the 1837 rebellion in Canada?

▷ *Durham Report*
(full name: "Report on the Affairs of British North America," 1839. Prepared by John George Lambton Durham)

Q Which British monarch ruled over Canada the longest – a reign of almost 64 years?

▷ *Queen Victoria (she ruled from 1837 – 1901)*

Q Canadian Indian Treaty Number One involved Indians of which province?

▷ *Manitoba*
(called the Stone Fort Treaty, it was signed on Aug. 3, 1871, with the Chippewa & Swampy Crees Indian tribes)

Q The province of Ontario boasts a total of 18 premiers since 1867. Alberta has had 10 since 1905. Which province has had only 2 premiers?

▷ *Newfoundland*

Q Since joining the rest of Canada, only two men have been elected to the province's highest political post. Who are they?

▷ *Joey Smallwood & Frank Moores*

Q Mr. Smallwood is the only living "Father of Confederation." The colorful politician was born in the small fishing village of Gambo on Christmas Eve, 1900. How many years did he serve as Newfoundland's premier?

▷ *23 years (1949 – 1972)*

Q Saskatchewan has had 11 premiers since it became a province back in 1905. Its first premier held office for 11 years. He shared his name with a famous Scottish poet and historical novelist who wrote the narrative poem about the Scottish Highlands called "The Lady of the Lake." What was the name of Saskatchewan's first premier?

▷ *Walter Scott*

Political Parties of Canada

I'll name the politician. You tell me the party he belonged or belongs to:

Q René Lévesque?

▷ *Parti Québecois*

Q St. Laurent?

▷ *Liberal*

Q Mackenzie King?

▷ *Liberal*

Q Ed Schreyer?

▷ *NDP*

Q Diefenbaker?

▷ *Conservative*

Going Back in Time

Q A first! It happened in the year 1623 and the event made many people happy! That was the year the first potatoes were grown in Canada. Where did they plant them and where were they grown?

▷ *Port Royal/Annapolis Royal, Nova Scotia*

Q On Christmas Eve, 1771, an employee of the Hudson's Bay Company discovered Great Slave Lake. It was a moving Christmas experience for him. What was his name?

▷ *Samuel Hearne*

Q Young Sam and his party had set out about a year before – in December of 1770. What was their point of departure – in other words, from what location on Hudson Bay did they start out?

▷ *York Factory*

Q Discovering Great Slave Lake was an unexpected bonus. Hearne had set out to find a certain valuable mineral, said to be in great abundance at the mouth of a certain river. What was the mineral he was after?

▷ *Copper (at the mouth of the Coppermine River)*

Q Hearne made another trip west about three years after he found Great Slave Lake. While on this trip, he founded Cumberland House. On the shores of what river was that post established?

▷ *The Saskatchewan River*

Q By the way, the success of Hearne's Arctic excursion was due, in no small measure, to the help and guidance he was given by a remarkable Indian who had eight wives. The women worked in the camps while Hearne and his friend hunted for food. What was the name of his faithful Indian companion?

▷ *Matonabbee (pronounced Mat-ton-à-bee)*

Q Monday, December 15th, 1890, a prominent North American leader was shot and killed. His people called him "Tatanka Yotanka." By what name do we know him best?

▷ *(Chief) Sitting Bull*

Q Sitting Bull was given the name "Tatanka Yotanka" when he was a teenager. He was 14 when he did something to one of his enemies, a feat that gained him the admiration of his elders, and which also earned him the name. What was that feat?

▷ *He scalped his opponent.*

Q After Sitting Bull's involvement in the battle of Little Big Horn, in which General Custer and his men were annihilated, Sitting Bull and his followers headed for Canada. He arrived in this country with 500 braves, 1,000 women and 3,500 horses! They settled at Wood Mountain on the Alberta/Saskatchewan border. The place they chose is now a Provincial Park. What is its present name?

▷ *Cypress Hills (Provincial Park)*

Q Not long after the Sioux' arrival in Canada, a major in the North West Mounted Police visited the camp, in an attempt to persuade the Chief and his people to return to the U.S. where the government had promised forgiveness and reservation land. What was the surname of the major who talked with the Chief?

▷ *Major Walsh*

Q But Sitting Bull was not easily persuaded. He remained until 1881, when his people were compelled to return to their homeland. It wasn't the police who forced their departure – but a calamity that affected every man, woman and child in the camp. What was that problem?

▷ *Starvation*

Q On Friday, December 12th, 1901, Cornwall, England and St. John's, Newfoundland shared an exciting moment in history. What was the unique accomplishment that gave the two widely-separated places something in common?

▷ *Marconi's wireless success*
(the signal was emitted from Poldhu, Cornwall; received at Signal Hill, St. John's)

97

Q In order to receive the signals transmitted from overseas, Marconi had to raise an aerial, the higher the better. So, he raised a copper aerial. He didn't build a tower, but how did he get the aerial to the desired height?

▷ *He used a box kite.*

Q How high did his aerial extend? Was it: 200 ft., 400 ft., or 600 ft.?

▷ *400 ft. high*

Q In order to hear the faint clicking of Cornwall's signal, Marconi ran his copper wire directly to a device that had been invented about a quarter of a century earlier, in 1876. What was this device?

▷ *A telephone*

Q The signal Marconi heard through that telephone was in Morse Code. Three dots were transmitted over and over again for a specified three-hour period, each day. What letter of the alphabet was being sent across the Atlantic?

▷ *The letter "S"*

Q Marconi's genius was clearly recognized. In 1909, he was appointed to the Italian Senate, and during the same year, another great honor was bestowed on him – outside of his native land. What was that honor?

▷ *He received the Nobel Prize (for physics)*

The Pioneer Press

Q On Wednesday, Nov. 14th, 1922, this country's most colorful newspaperman, the editor of the "Wetaskiwin Free Lance" signed "30" to his own life story. Name him.

▷ *Robert C. "Bob" Edwards*

Q Bob Edwards' "Wetaskiwan Free Lance" was the first paper to be published between Calgary and Edmonton. But his most famous newspaper originated in High River in 1902, and he later moved it (name and all) to Calgary. What was the name of that paper?

▷ *"The Calgary Eye Opener"*

Q The "Eye Opener" contained a distinctive brand of wit and sarcasm typical of its editor. For example, in one of his editorials, he wrote: "Now I know what a statesman is; he's a dead politician. We need more statesmen." Speaking of statesmen, Bob Edwards had a favorite pastime in common with Sir John A. Macdonald. What was it?

▷ *They both enjoyed their whiskey.*

Q In that regard, Mr. Edwards' integrity as a newspaperman was clearly evident as Alberta prepared to vote on Prohibition. His paper came out positively on the side of the prohibitionists! In what year did Alberta vote on this issue?

▷ *1915*

Q In addition to his fondness for whiskey, Bob Edwards had something else in common with Canada's first prime minister. They were both born in the same country. Name the country.

▷ *Scotland (Macdonald was born in Glasgow; Edwards was born in Edinburgh)*

New France

Q Prior to 1663, New France had failed to prosper as a colony. In that year, a new colonial policy came into being. Which French monarch was responsible for this new policy?

▷ *King Louis XIV (called "Louis the Great" or "The Grand Monarch")*

Q Louis was King, but the growth of the colony was largely due to the work of his capable Finance Minister. Who was he?

▷ *Jean Baptiste Colbert (1619–1683)*
(served as Superintendent of Finance for 25 years)

Q What is the name given to the kind of economic system under which Colbert established the colony and maintained it?

▷ *The Mercantile System (Mercantilism)*
(a regulating system for agriculture, industry and commerce set up to create a favorable balance of trade)

Q After 1663, a Sovereign or Superior Council was established to govern the colony. What were the three positions established on that council?

▷ *Governor/Bishop/Intendant*

Q Who were the three members who made up the First Council?

▷ *Governor (Louis de Buade, Comte de Palluau et) Frontenac*
Bishop (Francois Xavier de) Laval (de Montigny)
Intendant (Jean) Talon

1812!

Q There is a tall monument (185 ft. high), standing above Queenston Heights overlooking the Niagara River. Who does it commemorate?

▷ *General Sir Isaac Brock*

Q General Brock was a perfect target for one of the sharpshooting American invaders because he was wearing a brilliantly decorated sash. It was a gift he had received from a man who admired Brock greatly. Who was he?

▷ *Tecumseh (At the earlier battle of Detroit, Brock and Tecumseh rode side by side. Brock took off his sash and gave it to Tecumseh with a brace of silver-mounted pistols in token of his admiration. Tecumseh at once unwound his own sash and gave it to Brock who wore it with his uniform till the day he fell at Queenston.)*

101

Q Brock was killed in an attempt to remove the Americans from the crest of the hill. The scarlet jacket he was wearing at the time of his death is on display – bullet hole and all – in one of Ottawa's famous buildings. Which is it?

⇨ *National Library & Archives (not the War Museum)*

Q There is another outstanding historic site in Queenston. It is the home of another well-known figure associated with the War of 1812. Whose home is it?

⇨ *Laura Secord ('s)*

The Queen of Canada.

In 1953, the Canadian Parliament approved the following as the official title for the Queen: "Elizabeth the Second, by the Grace of God, of the United Kingdom, Canada, and Her other Realms and Territories, Queen, Head of the Commonwealth, Defender of the Faith."

Q In what year did Elizabeth Alexandra Mary ascend the throne?

⇨ *1952 (upon the death of her father, George VI, on Feb. 6, 1952)*

Q Both Queen Elizabeth and Prince Philip are great-great-grandchildren of which queen?

⇨ *Queen Victoria*

Q Queen Elizabeth and Prince Philip have four children. Name them.

> *Prince Charles (Philip Arthur George)*   *(born 1948)*
> *Princess Anne (Elizabeth Alice Louise)*   *(born 1950)*
> *Prince Andrew (Christian Edward)*   *(born 1960)*
> *Prince Edward (Antony Richard Louis)*   *(born 1964)*

Q Since Confederation, how many ruling monarchs (including Queen Elizabeth) has Canada had?

> *Six*
> *Victoria, 1837–1901; Edward VII, 1901–10;*
> *George V, 1910–36; Edward VIII, 1936;*
> *George VI, 1936–52 & Elizabeth II.*

Medals and Brass

Q The Victoria Cross is the highest award for valor given in the Commonwealth. What is the highest award for civilian bravery?

> *The George Cross*
> *(instituted in 1940 by George VI in recognition of the part played by civilians in modern warfare)*

Q The letters "C.B." are the common abbreviation for which conferred title of honor?

> *Companion of the Order of the Bath*
> *(the lowest order of the Bath; the others are Knight Commander and Knight Grand Cross)*

Q In which year did the Federal Government create the Order of Canada to honor those who have made significant contributions to the country?

⟁ *1967*

Q Which Canadian military decoration was created in 1972 "to honor professional excellence and exceptional devotion to duty"?

⟁ *The Order of Military Merit (for regular and reserve forces members)*

Canadian Politics

Q What party formed the government of Saskatchewan after the 1944 election?

⟁ *Co-operative Commonwealth Federation (CCF) (led by T.C. Douglas)*

Q Which Saskatchewan premier became the first leader of the federal New Democratic Party?

⟁ *Thomas Clement "Tommy" Douglas (at its founding convention in Ottawa in 1961)*

Q Who was elected CCF national leader in 1960?

⟁ *Hazen Argue (He was the last leader of the CCF In July, 1961, Douglas became leader, and the party became the NDP. On Feb. 18th, 1962, Argue left the NDP and joined the Liberal party)*

Q Which Liberal leader became premier of Saskatchewan after the 1964 elections?

▷ *Wilbert Ross Thatcher*

Quebec Separatism

Q Which former federal Social Credit M.P. formed the merger of the "Creditistes" and the "Ralliement pour Nationale"?

▷ *Gilles Gregoire*

Q What is the main separatist party in Quebec today called?

▷ *Parti Québecois (since 1968)*

Q Who is the author of *An Option for Quebec*?

▷ *René Lévesque (published in 1968)*

Dates in Canadian Politics

Often in Canadian history, the outcome of elections has been decided by one major issue. Give me the year of the election in which the following were issues in either federal or provincial history.

Q In this year, Albertans went to the polls to vote for a so-called "new economic order." They elected the first Social Credit government in history under the leadership of William Aberhart.

▷ *1935*

Q The unpopularity of Sir Wilfrid Laurier's Reciprocity Agreement with the United States brought down his Liberal government of fifteen years.

▷ *1911 (from 1896)*

Q Rising unemployment and the worst recession in Canadian history, led to the election of Viscount Richard Bedford Bennett as prime minister of Canada.

▷ *1930 (until 1935)*

Q In this election Sir Robert Laird Borden's Union Party carried the nation on the issue of conscription.

▷ *1917 (P.M. from 1911–1920; he won his first term as a result of the people's opposition to the Reciprocity Agreement)*

Q As a result of the referendum in this year, Newfoundlanders finally voted to join Confederation.

▷ *1948 (Nfld. officially joined Confederation on April 1st, 1949)*

Q Governor General Byng's failure to dissolve Parliament at the prime minister's request led to Mackenzie King's resignation as prime minister, and a brief Conservative government under Arthur Meighen. Unable to maintain power, the Conservatives also resigned. Give the date of the election that followed; the issue was constitutional prerogative.

▷ *1926 (in September) (King and the Liberal party won)*

Q The election of Jean Lesage following the death of Maurice Duplessis, began a movement in Quebec politics called the "Quiet Revolution". In what year was this election?

▷ *1960 (July 5th) (Lesage was premier until 1966)*

Q In this year, only one year after their victory at the polls, a Conservative government resigned on the issue of political corruption in what became known as the "Pacific Scandal."

▷ *1873*
(On April 2, 1873, in the House of Commons, the Hon. L.S. Huntington (Lib.) charged the Macdonald government with having awarded the contract for the building of the CPR to Sir Hugh Allan in return for contributions to party funds. The investigation led to the government's resignation on Nov. 5, 1873, and in the election in Jan. 1874, the Conservatives were soundly beaten.)

Acadia

Q "Evangeline" is the name of a long, narrative poem by Henry Wadsworth Longfellow (1807–1847), telling the tragic tale of two lovers (Evangeline & Gabriel) and what major theme?

▷ *Expulsion of the French Acadian colony ("Evangeline" first appeared in 1847)*

Q When the British took over the former French colony of Acadia in the early 1700s, little changed in the lives of the Acadians. However, the French doggedly refused to do what for the British?

▷ *They refused to take the Oath of Allegiance*

Q Little trouble occurred until the French began to fortify Louisburg and Beauséjour. It now seemed that the Acadian population, along with the French nationals, would become a threat to New England, and to which British settlement founded in 1749?

▷ *Halifax (Edward Cornwallis and some 2,500 colonists arrived at that time)*

Q Again the British, realizing the perilous situation, decided to enforce the oath on the Acadian population. They refused unless they would be exempted from military service. In July 1755, the Acadians were moved out to be dispersed throughout the British colonies. The number of Acadians moved was close to: 14,000, 44,000 or 104,000?

▷ *(Estimated at about) 14,000*

Q Today, which province has the largest population of Acadian descendants?

▷ *New Brunswick*

Canadian Law

Q From what source is the Civil Code of Quebec derived?

▷ *French Civil Law ("Coutume de Paris"/Code Napoleon) (also the Civil Code of the Canton of Vaud or of Sardinia; also Civil Code of Louisiana)*

Q In Canada, what branch of the law is under the jurisdiction of the federal Parliament?

▷ *Criminal Law (B.N.A. Act, section 91)*

Q What was the legislation called which was used in the 1920s and part of the 1930s, in Canada and the U.S., to prevent sale and consumption of alcoholic beverages?

▷ *Prohibition*

Q Who is the present Chief Justice of the Supreme Court?

▷ *(The Rt. Hon.) Bora Laskin, P.C.*

Q What does it mean when the Supreme Court declared a law to be "ultra vires" (pronounced weer-aze)?

▷ *It is "outside the jurisdiction" of the enacting body. (from Latin "vis", "vires", equally powers or strength; "ultra", beyond)*

Canada's Parliament

Q As originally set up in 1867, which Canadian parliamentary body was allowed 72 members?

▷ *Senate (Upper House) (24 each for Ontario, Quebec and the Maritimes)*

Q How many seats has the Canadian Senate?

▷ *102*

Q Which province has 10 Senators?

▷ *New Brunswick/Nova Scotia*

Q Which province has 4 Senators?

▷ *Prince Edward Island*

Q Which province is represented by 24 Senators?

▷ *Ontario/Quebec*

Q How many Senators represent each of the western provinces?

▷ *Six (each)*
(Manitoba, Saskatchewan, Alberta, & British Columbia)
(Newfoundland also has six Senators)

Siege of Quebec, 1759

Q The carefully planned British expedition against Quebec had General James Wolfe in command of the army. Who was commander-in-chief of the fleet?

▷ *Admiral (Sir) Charles Saunders*

Q What is the French name for the cove that provided the only feasible approach to the Plains of Abraham?

▷ *Anse Au Foulon (now Wolfe's Cove)*

Q Both Montcalm and Wolfe died in the battle over Quebec. Who succeeded General Wolfe?

▷ *General James Murray*

Q What treaty brought the Seven Years War to an end in 1763?

▷ *The Treaty of Paris (1763)*

British Control in Quebec after 1759

Q Who was the first British governor in Quebec?

▷ *General James Murray*
(Governor from 1760 to 1768 – he left Canada in 1766 but retained his title until 1768)

Q What group of British people in Quebec wanted a legislative assembly that would religiously exclude the French Canadians, and establish English civil law?

▷ *Merchants/Seigneurs*

Q Frontier expansion by the British in an area west of the Alleghany Mountains precipitated an Indian uprising. Which Ottawa Indian chief led this uprising?

▷ *Pontiac (the uprising is sometimes called "Pontiac's Conspiracy")*

Q Governor Murray's sympathy for the French Canadians put him in direct conflict with the British mercantile interests. Who replaced Murray in 1766, when he was recalled to England?

▷ *Sir Guy Carleton (1st Baron Dorchester)*

Running the Country

Q What is Canada's federal system of Government called?

⇨ *Constitutional Monarchy/Parliamentary System*

Q What statement is normally read at the opening of each session of Parliament?

⇨ *Speech from the Throne*

Q Who normally reads the Speech from the Throne?

⇨ *The Governor General*

Q Who prepares the Speech?

⇨ *The prime minister's staff (it is then approved by his Cabinet)*

Q For the first time in Canadian history, the speech was read by a reigning sovereign. In what year did this occur?

⇨ *1957 (October 1957, Queen Elizabeth II)*

Q In reply to the Speech from the Throne, within how many days must the federal parliamentary debate be completed?

⇨ *10 days*

Q In the Canadian Constitution, the power of unlimited taxation belongs to which level of government?

▷ *Federal/National*
(the provinces are limited to imposition of direct taxes)

Arctic Exploration

Q What Englishman, in 1607, sailed north along Greenland's east coast to Cape Hold-With-Hope, and on his return trip, discovered Hudson's Touches?

▷ *Henry Hudson (died 1611) (on this voyage, he sailed in the "Hopewell")*

Q What Danish navigator, in 1728, proved Asia and America were separate, by sailing through the strait?

▷ *Vitus Bering (1680–1741)*
(at Bering Strait, Alaska and Asia are only 56 miles apart)

Q What Norwegian explorer first sailed the Northwest Passage in 1903–1906?

▷ *Roald Amundsen (1872–1928)*
(He also navigated the Northeast Passage between 1918 & 1920)

Q What two Americans were, in 1926, the first men to fly over the North Pole?

⟡ *Rear Admiral Richard Evelyn Byrd (1888–1957) and Floyd Bennett (1890–1928)*
(Bennett piloted the aircraft from Spitbergen [now Svalbard] to the North Pole on May 9, 1926)
(They received Congressional Medals of Honor for their flight)

French-English Rivalry in North America Prior to 1759

Q Which fort, built by the English on the south shore of Lake Ontario, close to the beginning of the St. Lawrence, was erected on soil previously considered to be French?

⟡ *Fort Oswego*
(later it was to be the site of a major battle in the War of 1812)

Q Which leader of the reconstructed British government was determined to clear the French from the path of the expansion of the British colonies?

⟡ *William Pitt (The Elder) (1708–1778)*

Q What European war was being fought at almost the same time war broke out in North America?

⟡ *Seven Years War (1756–1763)*
(In America, it was called the French and Indian War.)

Q In the summer of 1758, two generals combined forces to capture the fortress of Louisbourg. One of the generals was Wolfe. Who was the other?

▷ *(British) General (Lord Jeffery) Amherst (1717–1797)*

Canada and the American Revolution

Q Which American general commanded the expedition of November 1775, that captured Montreal?

▷ *Brigadier-General Richard Montgomery (1738–1775)*

Q General Montgomery joined forces with another American general in an attempt to capture the citadel of Quebec. Who was the other general?

▷ *General Benedict Arnold (1741–1801)*

Q In 1791, Quebec was divided into two separate districts. What was the name of the act through which this division was carried out?

▷ *Canada Act/Constitutional Act*
(The districts were: Lower Canada, now Quebec, and Upper Canada, now Ontario, with the Ottawa River as the dividing line. This was the first official recognition of the name "Canada".)

Q Who was the first governor of Upper Canada?

▷ *Colonel John Graves Simcoe (1752–1806)*

Canada's Allies

Military alliances are often controversial, especially in peacetime.

Q What alliance of 15 western nations of which Canada was an original member, was formed on April 4th, 1949, for the co-operative protection of the North Atlantic?

⟳ *North Atlantic Treaty Organization (NATO)*

Q What was the original treaty called?

⟳ *The North Atlantic Pact*
(signed by Belgium, Canada, Denmark, France, Great Britain, Iceland, Italy, Luxembourg, the Netherlands, Norway, Portugal & the U.S. – Greece, Turkey & West Germany joined later)

Q What is the supreme body of NATO?

⟳ *North Atlantic Council*

Q What country, in 1966, withdrew from the integrated military structure of NATO, and does not participate in the Defence Planning Committee?

⟳ *France*

The Federal Government of Canada

You and your peers are the government of the near future. Let's see how well you understand how the Federal Government works before you get there.

Q Traditionally, how many years does the Governor General serve?

⟿ *Usually 5, sometimes extended to 7 years*

Q What kind of bill cannot be introduced in the Senate, but must originate in the Commons?

⟿ *Money/Financial Bills*
(for raising or spending money – as per B.N.A. Act: section 53)

Q Who is responsible for recommending appointments to the Senate?

⟿ *The Prime Minister*

Q What body has the primary task of applying the law, and carrying out the instructions of the cabinet?

⟿ *Civil Service*

Border-Crossing

Q Which war treaty established the Canada-U.S. border between the Atlantic Ocean and the Lake of the Woods area?

▷ *The Treaty of Paris (of 1783)*

Q In what year was the 49th parallel accepted as the boundary from the Lake of the Woods westward to the Pacific coast at the Straits of Juan de Fuca?

▷ *1846 (The Oregon Treaty)*

Q Which treaty resolved the boundary dispute between Main and New Brunswick?

▷ *The Ashburton-Webster Treaty (of 1842)*

Q In 1871, in order to finally settle the Pacific controversy, Wilhelm I, the German Emperor, arbitrated in favor of the U.S. for the ownership of which island?

▷ *San Juan Island*

Q The United States purchased Alaska in 1867. However, the boundary dispute wasn't settled until what year?

▷ *1903*
(by a joint commission of "six impartial jurists of repute" but many felt Canada had been betrayed by Lord Alverstone)

National Emblems

Although our national emblems are things we take largely for granted, they are an important part of our national heritage.

Q What is the top-most feature of the armorial bearings of Canada?

▷ *(The Imperial) Crown*

Q What king proclaimed these armorial bearings for Canada?

▷ *George V (from a Royal Proclamation dated Nov. 21, 1921)*

Q What monarch granted a coat of arms to Ontario in 1868?

▷ *Queen Victoria (in a Royal Warrant dated May 26, 1868)*

Q In what aspect are the coats of arms of Ontario and Quebec the same?

▷ *Both have a sprig of three maple leaves.*

Q What common feature surmounts the three provincial shields of Ontario, Manitoba and Alberta?

▷ *Red Cross of St. George*

Q Did Canada ever have ambitions to extend itself as an empire in the Caribbean?

⇨ *As a matter of fact – yes! On January 10th, 1974, Bill C-249 was introduced in Canada's House of Commons to study the feasibility of a union between Canada and chain of Caribbean Islands, the Turks and Caicos Islands.*

Q Who introduced the bill?

⇨ *Max Saltsman (NDP member for Waterloo-Cambridge)*

Q Such a bill usually has little chance of serious debate. What type of bill was it?

⇨ *Private Member's Bill*

Q Of what country were the Turks and Caicos Islands a colony at the time?

⇨ *British Crown Colony (part of British West Indies)*

Q What is the population of this island group? 11,000, 8,500, or 6,000 (approximately)?

⇨ *6,000*

The Canadian Coat of Arms

The original Canadian coat of arms featured the arms of the original four provinces. However, it soon became cluttered as new provinces joined Confederation.

Q The arms of which four countries are displayed on the current Canadian coat of arms?

⇨ *England/Scotland/Ireland/France*

Q In the arms, the supporters are a lion and a unicorn. What is the unicorn bearing?

⇨ *The ancient banner of France/the fleur-de-lis*

Q In Latin, what is the motto presented on the coat of arms?

⇨ *"A Mari Usque ad Mare" (from sea to sea)*

Q Above the shield is a crowned lion. What is he holding?

⇨ *A red maple leaf*

Canadian Symbols

Here's a flower, a description of a coat of arms or provincial shield. You tell me the province it represents.

Q The flower which is representative of this province is the white trillium:

⇨ *Ontario*

Q This province's flower is the white garden lily:

⇨ *Quebec*

Q The floral emblem of this province is the prairie lily:

▷ *Saskatchewan*

Q This provincial floral emblem is the dogwood:

▷ *British Columbia*

Q The shield is surmounted by the Cross of St. George, and it has a golden field of wheat:

▷ *Alberta*

Q The black galley on the shield symbolizes this province's seafaring traditions:

▷ *New Brunswick*

Q The shield of this province is occupied by two golden-crowned lions, and two silver unicorns:

▷ *Newfoundland*

Q The shield has a buffalo standing on a rock, surmounted by the Cross of St. George:

▷ *Manitoba*

Facts & Figures

Canadian Currency

Q What ship is on the Canadian dime?

⇨ *The "Bluenose"*
The 142-foot sailing schooner the Bluenose, the fastest sailing ship of its class, was built in the famous shipyards of Lunenburg, N.S. and launched on March 26, 1921. The schooner was sold in 1942 and became a West Indies freighter, foundering on a reef off Haiti in 1946. The dime first carried the "Bluenose" in 1937 and a 1929 50-cent stamp also commemorated the ship. A 1963 replica, also built in Lunenburg, was given to the Nova Scotia government in 1971.

Q On what piece of currency were the Mounties honoured for their centennial (1873–1973)?

⇨ *25c piece*

Q On what bill does a portrait of Sir John A. Macdonald appear?

⇨ *$10*

Q On what bill does a portrait of Sir Wilfrid Laurier appear?

⇨ *$5*

Q The Queen's portrait appears on many of our stamps, coins and bills. What is significant about 1977 for her?

⇨ *25th year as Queen*

Q What is depicted on the back of the 1967 $1.00 bill?

⇨ *Parliament buildings in Ottawa; logging on the Ottawa River; Parliamentary Library*

Theatre

Name the major professional theatre in the following Canadian cities:

Q Halifax?

⇨ *Neptune Theatre*

Q Edmonton?

⇨ *Citadel Theatre*

Q Winnipeg?

⇨ *Manitoba Theatre Centre*

Q Regina?

⇨ *Globe Theatre*

Metric System

Get your pens and paper ready for these problems dealing with the Metric System.

Q How many centimetres are there in three inches?

▷ *7.62 cm. (3 x 2.54)*

Q How many grams are there in two pounds?

▷ *907.2 grams (2 x 453.6)*

Q How many U.S. liquid quarts are there in three litres?

▷ *3.168 quarts (3 x 1.056)*

Q Convert six feet to centimetres:

▷ *182.8 cm. (6 x 30.48)*

Q Convert 77 degrees Fahrenheit to degrees Centigrade.

▷ *25 degrees C. ($\frac{5}{9}$ x (77-32))*

Q How many kilometres in three miles?

▷ *4.827 km. (3 x 1.609)*

Q Two hectares equals how many acres?

> ▷ *4.942 acres (2 x 2.471)*

Q How many cubic feet are there in four cubic metres?

> ▷ *141.26 cubic ft. (4 x 35.315)*

Canadian Films

Every year, the Academy Awards make news headlines in the United States and Canada. Canadian Film Awards are largely ignored. I hope you're up on your Canadian cinema!

Q What lovely actress starred in the 1973 film, "Kamouraska"?

> ▷ *Geneviève Bujold (directed by Claude Jutra)*

Q For his acting in what film did Gordon Pinsent win the 1972 best actor award?

> ▷ *"The Rowdyman" (which he also wrote)*

Q What French film won the 1971 award for best picture – about a young man's uncle?

> ▷ *"Mon Oncle Antoine" (directed by Claude Jutra)*

Q In 1972, what best picture was concerned with a wedding?

▷ *"Wedding in White" (writer-director: William Fruet)*

Q The 1969 best picture award went to a film entitled "The Best Damn Fiddler From. . . ." where to where?

▷ *"The Best Damn Fiddler From Calabogie to Kaladar" (an N.F.B. entry; screenplay by Joan Finnegan)*

Q What Canadian movie by Ted Kotcheff starred Richard Dreyfuss?

▷ *"The Apprenticeship of Duddy Kravitz"*

Q Who won the 1975 best actor award for his work in the film "Why Rock the Boat"?

▷ *Stuart Gillard*

Q What Canadian actress won the 1975 best actress award for her work in the films "Black Christmas" and "A Quiet Day in Belfast"?

▷ *Margo Kidder*

Q The 1975 best picture award went to what film?

▷ *"Les Ordres"*

Q Marilyn Lightstone won the best actress award for her work in the 1976 film which won best picture award – what was the film?

▷ *"Lies My Father Told Me"*

Facts about Canada

Q Which provincial name is derived from the Indian name for the longest river in the prairie provinces?

▷ *Saskatchewan (the name is derived from the Cree "kisiskatchewan," meaning "rapid river")*

Q The Second Prairie Level is also known by what other name?

▷ *The Saskatchewan Plain*

Q The "Regina Manifesto" formed the platform for which political party?

▷ *The Co-operative Commonwealth Federation (CCF) (founded August 1st, 1933)*

Q The "Farmer-Labor Party" later became known by what name?

▷ *The Co-operative Commonwealth Federation (CCF)*

Q In what city was the universal and international Exhibition held in 1967?

⇨ *Montreal (Quebec) ("Expo 67" – "Man and his World")*

I'll give you an important event of the 20th century. You tell me the decade in which the event took place.

Q In which decade did Lester Bowles Pearson win the Nobel Peace Prize?

⇨ *Fifties (in 1957, for organizing a U.N. force in Egypt)*

Q When did Canada get a distinctive national flag of its own?

⇨ *Sixties (proclaimed February 15th, 1965)*

Standard Time

Q The international dateline generally corresponds with the 180th meridian that runs across the Pacific, exactly half way around the world from Greenwich, England. Reckoning from Greenwich, how many standard time zones does Canada have?

⇨ *Seven:*
Newfoundland Standard
Atlantic Standard
Eastern Standard
Central Standard
Mountain Standard
Pacific Standard
Yukon Standard

132

Q How many standard earth meridians (or time zones) are there?

▷ *Twenty-four*

Q If it is 1:30 P.M. in St. John's, Newfoundland, what time is it in Halifax, Nova Scotia?

▷ *1:00 P.M.*
(there is a half-hour difference between Newfoundland and the Atlantic Standard times)

Q If it is 4:00 A.M. in Vancouver, what time is it in St. John's, Newfoundland?

▷ *8:30 A.M.*
(Vancouver is Pacific Standard Time, or 8 hours "slow"; Nfld. Standard Time is 3-1/2 hours "slow")

Q If it is 7:00 A.M. in Toronto, what time is it in Edmonton?

▷ *5:00 A.M.*
(Edmonton is Mountain Standard Time, 2 hours slower than Eastern Standard Time in Toronto)

I'll give you a Canadian city, and you tell me what time it is there when it is 12 noon at Greenwich. One hint: it would be 7 A.M. in Ottawa.

Q Montreal?

▷ *7:00 A.M.*

Q Halifax?

> *8:00 A.M.*

Q Toronto?

> *7:00 A.M.*

Q Winnipeg?

> *6:00 A.M.*

Q Calgary?

> *5:00 A.M.*

Here's a warning . . . there's bad weather ahead!

Q What word, derived from the Arabic "mausim," meaning "a season," designates strong, seasonal winds?

> *Monsoon*

Q Name this whirling wind of exceptional violence, usually associated with thunderstorms.

> *Tornado/Cyclone*

Q What do we call the violent hurricanes which occur in the Chinese seas?

▷ *Typhoons*

Q In Canada, what is the severe weather condition called, that is characterized by low temperatures, violent winds, and enormous amounts of snow?

▷ *Blizzard*

Astronomy

Q What is the proper name for the lights show that sometimes appears in the skies of the Northern Hemisphere at night – also called the "Northern Lights"?

▷ *Aurora Borealis*

Q What is the name given to a similar lights show that appears in the Southern Hemisphere – also called the "Southern Lights"?

▷ *Aurora Australis*

Q What color is most commonly seen during an auroral display?

▷ *Green*
(caused by atomic oxygen)

Q The red colors in an auroral display are caused by what two molecular elements?

▷ *Oxygen & Nitrogen*

Q When two heavenly bodies are closely aligned when viewed from the earth, having the same ecliptic longitude, how are they described?

▷ *In conjunction*

Q This term is used to describe the situation of a planet when its celestial longitude differs by 180° from that of the sun.

▷ *In opposition*

Q What word describes the position of one heavenly body in relation to another 90° away—represented by a symbol that looks like a square?

▷ *Quadrature*

Q What word is commonly used to designate an occultation of a planet or star?

▷ *Eclipse (occultation: concealment; interception by intervention; obscurement)*

Measurement

International System – our new measurement system. You tell me what units serve as the basis of these elements of the international system.

Q What is the basic unit for the measurement of length?

▷ *Metre (counterpart of the yard)*

Q What is the basic unit for the measurement of time?

▷ *Second (in both the English and metric systems)*

Q What is the basic unit of measurement of electric current?

▷ *Ampere*
(defined as that current which would deposit 1.118 milligrams of silver per second in a specified voltameter)

Q What is the basic unit for the measurement of mass in the M.K.S. scientific system?

▷ *Kilogram (counterpart of pound)*
M.K.S. – meter-kilogram-second

Q What is the basic unit for the measurement of light intensity or luminance?

▷ *Candela/Candle (also International Candle)*
(therefore known as candle power)

Instruments of Measurement

You tell me what it measures.

Q What does a barometer measure?

⇨ *Atmospheric Pressure*

Q What does a seismometer measure?

⇨ *Earth Tremors (intensity, place, duration, direction, etc. of earth tremors)*

Q What does a zymometer measure?

⇨ *The process of fermentation*

Q What does a hygrometer measure?

⇨ *Atmospheric moisture/humidity (of air or gas)*

Q What does a sphygmomanometer measure?

⇨ *Blood Pressure (pronounced sfig-mom-a-nam-atur)*

Q What does a photometer measure?

⇨ *Intensity of light*

Q What does an altimeter measure?

⇨ *Height above the earth's surface/height above sea level*

Q What does an ammeter measure?

⇨ *Electric current*

What are the proper prefixes to represent the following?

Q Ten to the minus two – or one hundredth part:

⇨ *Centi (from the Latin word "centum" meaning "hundred")*

Q Ten to the minus sixth – or one millionth part:

⇨ *Micro (from the Greek word "mikros," meaning "small")*

Q A trillionfold – or ten to the twelfth:

⇨ *Tera (from Greek "teras," meaning "monster")*

Q Ten to the sixth – or a millionfold:

⇨ *Mega (from the Greek word "megas," meaning "large")*

Q Ten to the minus three – or the thousandth part:

⇨ *Milli (from Latin "mille," meaning "a thousand")*

Medical Abbreviations

Q Ad libitum – how often do you take this?

▷ *At one's pleasure*

Q How often must you take a medicine if the doctor has written t.i.d.?

▷ *Three times a day (Latin "ter in die")*

Q a.c. – as instructions about when to take the medicine?

▷ *Before meals (from Latin "ante cibos," meaning "before meals")*

Q What will the pharmacist give you if the doctor's orders call for "ung"?

▷ *Ointment/ungent/salve (from Latin "unguare," meaning "to anoint")*

Miscellaneous Facts and Figures

Q If a woodchuck can chuck one half chuck of wood in three-quarters of an hour, how many chucks can he chuck in an hour-and-a-half?

▷ *One full chuck (if a woodchuck could chuck wood)*

Q In reference to business, what is "vertical integration"?

▷ *Ownership of several branches of one industry*
(i.e.: owning car-manufacturing company as well as tire-
manufacturing company)

Q Who made the first non-stop flight across the Atlantic Ocean?

▷ *On June 14 & 15, 1919, Capt. John Alcock and Lieutenant*
Arthur S. Brown, British aviators, flew from Saint John's,
Newfoundland to Clifden, Ireland. It took 16 hours and 27
minutes.

Q Has man ever stopped Niagara Falls?

▷ *It is possible, and has been done. In June 1969, the United*
States Army Corps of Engineers, under the United States -
Canadian agreements, in an effort to prevent the creation of
navigational hazards by falling rocks, "shut off the Falls". A
dam was built across the Niagara River Channel about a half
mile upstream from the Falls, temporarily stopping them.

Q According to a popular ditty, whom did George Drew know?

▷ *My Father*
(George Alexander Drew was Premier of Ontario 1943 - 1948
and was appointed High Commissioner to England in 1957.)
(to the tune of "Onward Christian Soldiers"
"George Drew knew my father,
father knew George Drew")

Q Can you name one of four Canadians who have won the Nobel Prize?

> Frederick Banting (Medicine/Physiology, 1923)
> John J.R. Macleod (Medicine/Physiology, 1923)
> Lester B. Pearson (Peace, 1957)
> Gerhard Herzberg (Chemistry, 1971)

Q What are the remaining three categories in which Canada has never won a Nobel Prize?

> Physics, Literature & Economics

Q What Manitoba town was established by the International Nickel Company in the Moak Lake Area?

> Thompson (Manitoba)

Q Who was the first secular nurse in North America who founded the Hotel Dieu?

> Jeanne Mance (1606–1673)

Q For which Canadian province is Truro the transportation hub?

> Nova Scotia
> (originally called Cobequid, a Micmac term meaning "the end of the water's flow")

Q What type of hatchet derives its name from the Algonquin word meaning "to knock down"?

> Tomahawk (from "otomahuk")

Q Who was the first Canadian-born Governor General?

▷ *Vincent Charles Massey (Governor General from 1952–1959)*

Q In what year was the present Canadian flag officially adopted?

▷ *1965 (proclaimed Feb. 15, 1965)*

Q How many readings must a bill have in the House of Commons, before it is passed?

▷ *Three readings*

Q Who, in addressing a joint session of the Canadian Senate and House of Commons, said: "In three weeks England will have her neck wrung like a chicken. Some chicken! Some neck!"?

▷ *Sir Winston (Leonard Spencer) Churchill (1874–1965) (delivered December 30th, 1941)*

Q On which denomination of our present Canadian money do you find fishing trawlers featured?

▷ *The five-dollar bill*

Q Which Canadian province has the largest amount of coastline?

▷ *Newfoundland (& Labrador)*

Q What is the fastest, regularly-scheduled train in Canada?

⇨ *The "Turbo"*
(it travels between Toronto & Montreal – a distance of 335 miles in 4 hours and 10 mins.)

Q Which Canadian province has had the largest population since the Canadian census in 1971?

⇨ *Ontario*

Q Which Canadian province was named in honor of Queen Victoria's daughter?

⇨ *Alberta (in 1882) (she was Princess Louise Caroline Alberta)*

Q Which Canadian province was originally called "New Caledonia"?

⇨ *British Columbia*
(it was changed in 1858, at the suggestion of Queen Victoria)

Biology Quiz

Here are some Canadian mammals. Do you know what biological scientific order each belongs to?

Q A beaver is a gnawing mammal.

⇨ *Rodentia (Rodents)*

Q Bats are flying mammals.

⇨ *Chiroptera (meaning hand-winged)*

Q Wolves are meat-eating mammals.

⇨ *Carnivora (carnivorous)*

Q This animal is closely related to termites, ticks and scorpions. They are found almost everywhere in the world. They like to eat insects. What do we call them?

⇨ *Spiders*

Q You'll find this spider in parts of Alberta, Saskatchewan, British Columbia and Ontario. Its bite has killed a number of people in the U.S. over the years, but no Canadians have been victims. What spider is it?

⇨ *Black Widow (called the Black Widow because she spends a large part of her time as a widow after eating her mate)*

Q Although the bite of the female Black Widow can be fatal, only a certain percentage of those bitten die. What percentage? 10% – 20% – 40%?

⇨ *10%*

Q Where is the largest rodent community in Canada?

⇨ *It is reported to be a colony of prairie dogs in Saskatchewan. The community consists of burrows that cross-hatch an area covering 25,000 sq. miles, with a population of 400 million animals!*

Q What am I?

Clue I. When it comes to color – you'll find me in many shades all the way from a dark purple to a soft delicate pink! But even to those who love me – my appearance doesn't do much to tempt the palate.

Clue II. People love me in the province whose highest point of land is Mount Carleton! They eat me in all kinds of recipes – raw, toasted, powdered or mixed in soups and stews!

Clue III. Of my kind – I'm rated by many to be the best in the world! And my name is usually linked with a place called Black's Harbour where 40 tons of me is picked annually. What am I?

Clue IV. I'm rich in iron and iodine – I'm a tangy, salty seaweed – and any self respecting New Brunswicker will tell you I'm "a nourishing food that is second to none"!

 Dulse

Q To which mammalian family do the mink, marten, wolverine, ferret and skunk belong?

⬦ *The Weasel family/Mustelidae*
(also badgers, otters, polecats, ratels and tayras)

Words and Literature

Commonplace Canadian Names – their origins!

Q The city on the south bank of the Saguenay River near Chicoutimi – is called Arvida! It was founded in 1926 by the Aluminum Co. of Canada! Why did they choose the name Arvida – is it a chemical used in the processing of aluminum – is it a Greek word meaning "Great Promise" – or was it named after a man! Arvida?

▷ *After a man – in 1926 he was Alcan's President Ar(thur) Vi(ning) Da(vis)*

Q We've all heard about the CIA – the United States Central Intelligence Agency. But have you heard about the Canadian organization known as the C-I-I-A? It's not a secret agency – it's a very important Canadian Institute! Canadian Institute takes care of the first two letters C and I – but what do the last two letters I and A represent? The Canadian Institute of – what?

▷ *International Affairs*
(a private voluntary organization with over 20 branches founded in 1928 to encourage in Canada, research, discussion and publication in the field of international affairs)

Q Canada means many things to many people. Canada means our home and native land to many Canadians. But what does "canada" mean to the Portuguese? Is "canada" – a spicy cold plate served on religious holidays? Is it a "liquid measure" or is it a kind of medieval dance performed at rural weddings?

▷ *Liquid measure! When a man buying wine in Lisbon asks for a canada he gets exactly 1.38 litres!*

Words, Words, Words

Q In the jargon of the early unionists, these words were common – "fink" and "scab". They were names applied to men and women who would take the jobs of striking workers. Strong unionists didn't like men who were labelled "scissorbills". What was a "scissorbill"?

▷ *A laborer who was militantly anti-union*

Q What was the name applied to union men who were active and dedicated union members? Think of Canada's record-breaking unicycle rider from Alberta, Willy Watts. His nickname is close to the name we're after.

▷ *Wobbly (Good union workers were called "Wobblies" – the term came from an American revolutionary labor organization called the I.W.W. for industrial workers of the world or the "Wobblies".)*

Q It's the English word most frequently spoken in everyday conversation. What is it?

▷ *I!*

Q The word "tip" has a cloudy background. Some say it's a corruption of the word "stipend," meaning a small payment of money. The more popular guess is that the word "tip" is made up of the first letters of the three words posted on coin boxes on the tables of coffee houses in Dr. Samuel Johnson's day. What three words?

> *To insure promptness*

Q A word used as slang, especially by cab drivers, to describe poor tippers, is the name also applied to a pancake. It's not a "flannel cake" or a "griddle cake". What do cabbies in cities like Montreal and New York call a poor tipper?

> *Flapjack!*

How well do you know your Ps & Qs?
First, let's deal with the Ps!

Q The owner of a restaurant talks about his P and L. What exactly is he talking about? P and L stands for?

> *Profit & Loss*

Q Your mailman knows, but do you know what the letters PPD stand for?

> *Prepaid/Postpaid*

150

Q A conductor stands before the Toronto Symphony, about to conduct a symphonic work. One passage is marked PP. How must the passage be played? What does PP mean to a musician?

▷ *Pianissimo (means very softly)*

So much for the P's, now the Q's:

Q Q is one letter you won't find on your telephone dial. What is the other?

▷ *Z*

Q If A is number one in the alphabet, and Z is number 26, what number is Q?

▷ *17*

Q In Canada, you can find these letters painted on signs, buildings and automobiles. What do the letters QPP stand for?

▷ *Quebec Provincial Police*

Newspapers

What is the morning newspaper in each of the following Canadian cities?

Q Victoria?

⇨ *Daily Colonist*

Q Halifax?

⇨ *Chronicle-Herald*

Q Calgary?

⇨ *Albertan*

Q Toronto?

⇨ *Globe & Mail
Sun*

Q Vancouver?

⇨ *Province*

Q Moncton?

⇨ *Times*

Q Montreal? (English)

⇨ *Gazette*

Q What does "Le Devoir" mean?

▷ *It means "duty," or "task," and it also means French Canada's largest circulating daily newspaper, founded in 1910 by Henri (Joseph Napoleon) Bourassa (1868–1952). Bourassa was a Quebec Nationalist with a patriot's heritage. His grandfather was the rebel, Louis Joseph Papineau, the leader of the Lower Canada Rebellion of 1837. Henri was elected to Canada's House of Commons in 1896, where he became known as one of the greatest orators of his time. He became a great supporter of the Ligue Nationaliste, newly founded in 1903, and for 30 years, the leader of the French Canadian nationalist movement.*

The following are Canadian daily newspapers of large circulation. What cities do they serve?

Q The morning paper, the "Chronicle-Herald".

▷ *Halifax (Nova Scotia)*

Q The evening paper, the "Transcript".

▷ *Moncton (New Brunswick)*

Q What city is served by the evening "Leader-Post"?

▷ *Regina (Saskatchewan)*

Q The evening "Star-Phoenix".

▷ *Saskatoon (Saskatchewan)*

Q Finally, what is the Edmonton evening paper?

▷ *The "Journal"*

Canadian Authors

Q Who wrote:
Survival?

▷ *Margaret Atwood*

Q Wheels?

▷ *Arthur Hailey*

Q The Energy of Slaves?

▷ *Leonard Cohen*

Q A Whale for the Killing?

▷ *Farley Mowat*

Q Lives of Girls and Women?

▷ *Alice Munro*

Quotable Quotes by Canadians

Q Who said:
"Goods satisfactory or money refunded"?

▷ *Timothy Eaton*

Q "He flung himself from the room, flung himself upon his horse and rode madly off in all directions"?

▷ *Stephen Leacock*

Q "The medium is the message"?

▷ *Marshall McLuhan*

Q "All I know is that within every man and woman a secret is hidden, and as a photographer it is my task to reveal it if I can."?

▷ *Yousuf Karsh*

Q A famous English poet who was somewhat disillusioned about Canada, once wrote: "The only poet in Canada was very nice to me in Ottawa. Canada's a bloody place for a sensitive real poet like this to live all his life in." Who was this man, who is best remembered for his poem "The Soldier"?

▷ *Rupert Brooke*

Q In a book called *Sam Slick's Wise Saws*, there appears the famous quotation: "There's many a true word said in jest." Who wrote that?

⇨ *Thomas (T.C. Haliburton)*

Q A famous Canadian once wrote these lines:
I dreamed a dream when the woods were green,
And my April heart made an April Scene,
In the far, far distant land.
That even I might something do
That should keep my memory for the true
And my name from the spoiler's hand.

The poet was the victim of an assassin. Who was the author?

⇨ *D'Arcy McGee*

Literary Figures

Q He was born in England, was raised in Scotland, worked in Vancouver and wrote verses in Whitehorse and Dawson! He's known as "The Poet of the Yukon." What was his name?

⇨ *Robert Service*

Q In 1907 Robert Service wrote a collection of poems that included "The Shooting of Dan McGrew" & "The Cremation of Sam McGee". What was the name given to the collection including these and other works?

⇨ *Songs Of A Sourdough*

Q In "The Shooting of Dan McGrew" the first line sets the scene. We're told that "A bunch of the boys were whooping it up in the Malamute Saloon" – what exactly is a "malamute"?

▷ *A dog (a sled dog named after the Eskimo who bred them!)*

Q Robert Service was 84 when he died in 1958! And while he was born in England, was raised in Scotland, and gained international acclaim while living in Canada – he didn't find his final resting place in any of them! In what country is Mr. Service buried?

▷ *France (In Brittany)*

Q What literary giant am I?

Clue I. I was born December 30, 1869, in Swanmoor, Hants, England. I was educated at Upper Canada College, and at the Universities of Toronto and Chicago.

Clue II. I joined McGill University in 1903, and became a department head (of Political Science) until 1936.

Clue III. I wrote more than sixty books – one titled *Elements of Political Science*, which was published in 1906.

Clue IV. But it is as a humorist that I will likely be best remembered. My writings included *Literary Lapses* and *Sunshine Sketches of a Little Town*.

▷ *Stephen Butler Leacock*

Canadian Female Poets

The unique style of Canadian poetry has been greatly influenced by the sensitivity and insight of Canada's finest female poets.

Q Which Canadian female poet has published several collections of poetry, including *Passage of Summer: Selected Poems*, and is noted for her poems "Labor Day Week-End", "Gold Man" and "On El Greco's Painting of the Agony in the Garden"?

▷ *Elizabeth Brewster*

Q Gwendolyn MacEwen was awarded the Governor General's Award for Poetry in 1969 for which published collection of poems?

▷ *The Shadow Maker*

Q Which Canadian female poet has published poetry books entitled *The Enchanted Adder* and *The Power of the Dog*, and has written the play *One, Two, Three, Alary*?

▷ *Rona Murray (published "Selected Poems" in 1974)*

Q Which award-winning female poet wrote poems such as "Eden Is A Zoo", "A Dialogue" and "He Is Last Seen"?

▷ *Margaret Atwood*
(she won the Governor General's Award for Poetry in 1966)

Famous Canadian Authors

Q Who is the author of *The Stone Angel*?

⮞ *Margaret Lawrence*
(also author of A Jest of God & The Fire Dwellers)

Q *Ringing the Changes* is the autobiography of which well-known author?

⮞ *Mazo De la Roche (1885–1961) (it was published in 1957)*

Q Which Canadian author-broadcaster wrote, *Drifting Home*, an account of his attachment to Canada's North?

⮞ *Pierre Berton (published in 1973)*

Q *The Mayor of All the People* is the collected memoirs of which Canadian politician?

⮞ *Nathan Phillips*
(28 consecutive years on Toronto's city council, including 8 years as mayor)

Q Which Canadian artist's journals are collected in the book entitled, *Hundreds and Thousands*?

⮞ *Emily Carr (1871–1945) (published in 1966)*

Q On Friday, November 26th, 1943, one of this country's outstanding poets died in Toronto. He wrote the sonnet sequence "Songs Of The Common Day". Who was he?

▷ *Sir Charles G.D. Roberts*

Q While Sir Charles died in Toronto, he was born many miles east of there, in the year 1860. In what province was he born?

▷ *New Brunswick (near Fredericton)*

Q At 25, Roberts became Professor of English and French Literature at King's College, in 1885. In what province is King's College?

▷ *Nova Scotia*

Q The best feature of Sir Charles G.D. Roberts' work is to be found in his exact observations of two distinct aspects of nature in Canada. One was the landscape. What was the other?

▷ *Wildlife*

Q Sir Charles published this poem when he was 33. Can you give the title?

"When potatoes were in blossom,
When the new hay filled the mows,
Sweet the paths we trod together –
Bringing home the cows."

▷ *Bringing Home the Cows*

Word Games

Here are some Phobias. You tell me what fear they entail.

Q Hematophobia?

⟹ *Fear of blood*

Q Cynophobia?

⟹ *Fear of dogs/rabies*

Q Zoophobia?

⟹ *Fear of animals*

Q Acrophobia?

⟹ *Fear of heights*

Q Ornithophobia?

⟹ *Fear of birds*

Q Pyrophobia?

⟹ *Fear of fire/heat*

Q Agoraphobia?

⟹ *Fear of open spaces*

Q Astraphobia?

⇨ *Fear of thunder & lightning*

French Words

Which French word or phrase, commonly used in the English language, describes the following:

Q The expression that means composure, self-control and coolness?

⇨ *Sang-froid*

Q The ability to say and do the right thing in any situation?

⇨ *Savoir-faire*

Q The word that means dash, flare or verve?

⇨ *Panache*

Q An accomplished and presumably irreversible deed or fact?

⇨ *Fait accompli*

Works of English-Canadian Literature

Identify the Author of each:

Q Jalna

⟹ *Mazo De la Roche*
(published in 1927, it won the Atlantic Monthly
$10,000 prize)

Q Hesperus and Other Poems & Lyrics

⟹ *Charles Sangster (published in 1860)*

Q Sunshine Sketches of a Little Town

⟹ *Stephen Butler Leacock (published in 1912)*

Q They Shall Inherit the Earth

⟹ *Morley Edward Callaghan (published in 1935)*

Q Anne of Green Gables

⟹ *Lucy Maud Montgomery (published in 1908)*

Word Games

Q A North American slang word for a play which has failed; a large, festive bird?

⟶ *Turkey*

Q A fighting instrument used in medieval warfare; a long-snouted, freshwater game fish?

⟶ *Pike*

Q An important part of a hockey player's equipment; a large, flat-bodied sea animal?

⟶ *Skate*

Q A bold and dishonest person who is very adept at swindling; a large, voracious sea fish?

⟶ *Shark*

French-Canadian Literature

Identify the author of each of the following works:

Q Who wrote *Chez Nous*?

⟶ *Adjutor Rivard*
(published in French in 1914; translated by W.H. Blake in 1924)

164

Q Who is the author of *Bonheur d'Occasion* and *Alexandre Chenevert*?

▷ *Gabrielle Roy*

Q The first major French-Canadian historian, he produced *Histoire du Canada*, first published in 1845 – 48. It has since been reprinted several times.

▷ *François Xavier Garneau*

Q Who wrote *Maria Chapdelaine, Récit du Canada Français*?

▷ *Louis Hémon*
(Le Temps in Paris published it in installments in 1914)

Q Who is the author of *Au Pied de la Pente Douce* and *Les Plouffe*?

▷ *Roger Lemelin*

French-English

As students of French are aware, nouns are classified according to their gender. Here are certain French nouns and their English equivalent. Is the noun masculine or feminine?

Q Auto – French word for "automobile"?

▷ *Feminine (L'automobile)*

Q Papillon – French word for "butterfly"?

▷ *Masculine (Le papillon)*

Q Pomme – French word for "apple"?

▷ *Feminine (La pomme)*

Q Poisson – French word for "fish"?

▷ *Masculine (Le poisson)*

Q Mouche – French word for "fly"?

▷ *Feminine (La mouche)*

Translate the following French phrases into English:

Q Permettez-moi:

▷ *Allow me/Let me/Permit me*

Q Defense de crâcher:

▷ *No spitting (allowed)*

Q Bonne chance:

▷ *Good luck*

Q Comment cela:

⇨ *How's that?/What did you say?*

Q Bon Anniversaire:

⇨ *Happy Birthday*

Q Coureur de dot:

⇨ *Fortune-hunter*

Translate the following phrases used in French conversation into English:

Q Je désire téléphoner:

⇨ *I wish to (use the) telephone.*

Q La ligne est occupée:

⇨ *The line is busy.*

Q Où sont mes bagages?:

⇨ *Where are my suitcases/Where is my baggage/Luggage?*

Q Prenez à gauche:

⇨ *Take a left turn/Turn to the left.*

Q Je voudrais une chambre:

⇨ *I would like a room.*

Q Quel beau temps!:

⇨ *What fine weather!*

Q Une table pour deux, s'il vous plâit:

⇨ *A table for two, please.*

Q Où se trouve la ville?:

⇨ *Where is the town? (city?)*

Broadcasting in Canada

Over the past decade, broadcasting in Canada has become a major concern because of its significant cultural influence.

Q Which Canadian city heard the first broadcast of the human voice in the winter of 1919?

⇨ *Montreal (Marconi's radio station XWA)*

Q In what year did the first Canadian television broadcast occur?

⇨ *1952 (in Montreal and Toronto)*

Q In 1936, the federal government created the Canadian Broadcasting Corporation to replace which organization?

⇨ *Canadian Radio Broadcasting Commission (CRBC)*
(which had commenced operations in May of 1933)

Q The first transatlantic television was aided by which active satellite?

⇨ *Telstar I (in 1962)*
(built by Bell Telephone Laboratories; launched in July 1962; it relayed the first live TV picture – the American flag – across the Atlantic to receiving stations in England & France)

Canadian News Headlines

Q The 1891 news headline, "The Old Chieftain's Last Stand" refers to which Canadian politician?

⇨ *Sir John A. Macdonald*
(In the general election of 1891, he won the election, but his exertions during the course of it brought about a collapse from which he never really recovered.)

Q The 1946 headline, "40 to 50 Held In Spy Case – Russian Named By Minister," preceded the Royal Commission investigating spy activity. Identify the 27-year old Russian cipher clerk who sought asylum in Canada after presenting 109 valuable Russian Embassy documents to the authorities.

⇨ *Igor Gouzenko*

Q Who was the Canadian prime minister when the headline, "After Wild Session – New Storm Erupts over Pipeline Deal" hit the press?

▷ *Louis (Stephen) St. Laurent*
(Liberal prime minister from 1948 – 1957)

Q The "I'm Alone Incident" touched off an international crisis in 1929, among the United States and Canada, England and France. What happened in the "I'm Alone Incident"?

▷ *The United States Coast Guard sank the Canadian registered schooner "I'm Alone" as she sailed 200 miles beyond U.S. territorial limits. (The schooner was suspected of rum-running during the U.S. prohibition.)*